Introduction to *Daily Paragraph Editing*

Why *Daily Paragraph Editing*?

Daily Paragraph Editing is designed to help students master and retain grade-level skills in language mechanics and expression through focused, daily practice. Instead of practicing skills in a series of random, decontextualized exercises, *Daily Paragraph Editing* embeds language skills in paragraphs that represent the types of text that students encounter in their daily reading and writing activities across the curriculum. A weekly writing activity allows students to apply the skills they have been practicing throughout the week in their own short compositions.

What's in *Daily Paragraph Editing*?

Daily Paragraph Editing contains lessons for 36 weeks, with a separate lesson for each day.

Each week's lessons for Monday through Thursday consist of individual reproducible paragraphs that contain errors in the following skills:

- capitalization
- punctuation
- spelling
- language usage, and more

Student's daily lesson pages for Monday through Thursday include:

- a label indicating the type of writing modeled in the weekly lesson

- a paragraph with errors for students to correct; along with the other 3 paragraphs for the week, this forms a complete composition

- daily and weekly lesson identifiers

- as needed, the "Watch For" logo alerts students to more challenging skills to address in the paragraph

SOCIAL STUDIES ARTICLE: Kites—Not Just for Fun   Daily Paragraph Editing

Name _____

Kites—Not Just for Fun

People the world over has been flying kites for centuries in fact, kites were invented over two thousand years ago! one ancient story tells of a chinese general his army was trying to overthrow a cruel emperor. the general made a kite he tied a not in the string Next, his soldiers flew it in the direction of the palace When the kite was over the palace the general marked the string and reeled in the kite

WATCH FOR
• run-on sentences

MONDAY   WEEK 1

Students correct the errors in each daily paragraph by marking directly on the page. A reproducible sheet of Proofreading Marks (see page 10) helps familiarize students with the standard form for marking corrections on written text. Full-page Editing Keys show corrections for all errors in the daily paragraphs. Error Summaries help teachers identify the targeted skills in each week's lessons, and therefore help teachers plan to review or introduce the specific skills needed by their students.

Teacher's full-sized annotated Editing Key pages include:

- a label indicating the type of writing modeled in the weekly lesson

- the original student text with corrections marked in red (using the proofreading marks presented on page 10)

- daily and weekly lesson identifiers

- a summary of the errors in each paragraph to use in identifying unfamiliar skills to teach or review with students prior to assigning the paragraph. Some students may be more successful if you share the Error Summary with them before they read and edit the paragraph.

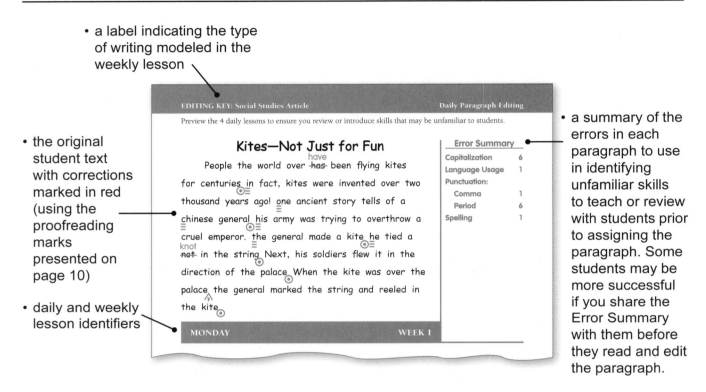

When corrected and read together, the four paragraphs for one week's lesson form a cohesive composition that also serves as a writing model for students. The weekly four-paragraph compositions cover a broad range of expository and narrative writing forms from across the curriculum, including the following:

- nonfiction texts on grade-level topics in social studies and science
- biographies, book reviews, editorials, instructions, interviews, journal entries, and letters
- fables, fantasy and science fiction, historical fiction, personal narratives, and realistic fiction

EMC 2727 • Daily Paragraph Editing • ©2004 by Evan-Moor Corp.

Each Friday lesson consists of a writing prompt that directs students to write in response to the week's four-paragraph composition. This gives students the opportunity to apply the skills they have practiced during the week in their own writing. Students gain experience writing in a wide variety of forms, always with the support of familiar models.

Friday writing prompts include:

- a prompt to write a composition in the same form as modeled in the weekly lesson

- sample topic sentences to support reluctant writers

- a weekly lesson identifier

- hints to help students address skills that are specific to the writing form

- a label indicating the type of writing modeled in the weekly lesson

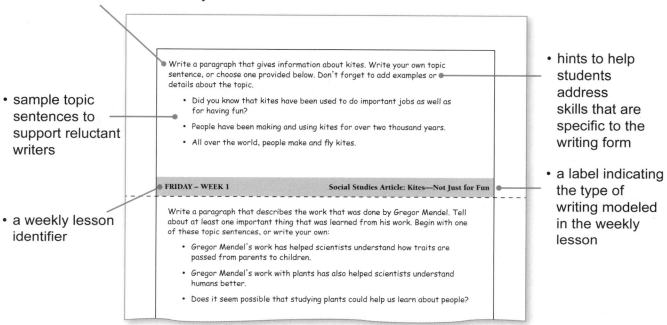

Write a paragraph that gives information about kites. Write your own topic sentence, or choose one provided below. Don't forget to add examples or details about the topic.

- Did you know that kites have been used to do important jobs as well as for having fun?
- People have been making and using kites for over two thousand years.
- All over the world, people make and fly kites.

FRIDAY – WEEK 1   Social Studies Article: Kites—Not Just for Fun

Write a paragraph that describes the work that was done by Gregor Mendel. Tell about at least one important thing that was learned from his work. Begin with one of these topic sentences, or write your own:

- Gregor Mendel's work has helped scientists understand how traits are passed from parents to children.
- Gregor Mendel's work with plants has also helped scientists understand humans better.
- Does it seem possible that studying plants could help us learn about people?

An Editing Checklist for students (see page 11) helps them revise their own writing or critique their peers' efforts. An Assessment Rubric (see page 9) is provided to help you assess student writing.

A reproducible student Language Handbook (pages 168–176) outlines the usage and mechanics rules for students to follow in editing the daily paragraphs. The Handbook includes examples to help familiarize students with how the conventions of language and mechanics are applied in authentic writing.

How to Use *Daily Paragraph Editing*

You may use *Daily Paragraph Editing* in several ways, depending on your instructional objectives and your students' needs. Over time, you will probably want to introduce each of the presentation strategies outlined below so you can identify the approach that works best for you and your students.

The four paragraphs that comprise each week's editing lessons include a set of errors that are repeated throughout all four paragraphs. We recommend that you provide a folder for students to keep their *Daily Paragraph Editing* reference materials and weekly lessons. It will work best to reproduce and distribute all four daily paragraphs for a given week on Monday. That way, students can use the previous days' lessons for reference as the week progresses.

Directed Group Lessons

Daily Paragraph Editing activities will be most successful if you first introduce them as a group activity. You might also have students edit individual copies of the day's lesson as you work through the paragraph with the group. Continue presenting the Monday through Thursday lessons to the entire class until you are confident that students are familiar with the editing process. Try any of the following methods to direct group lessons:

Option 1

1. Create and display an overhead transparency of the day's paragraph.

2. Read the paragraph aloud just as it is written, including all the errors.

3. Read the paragraph a second time, using phrasing and intonation that would be appropriate if all end punctuation were correct. (You may find it helpful to read from the Editing Key.) Read all other errors as they appear in the text.

4. Guide students in correcting all end punctuation and initial capitals in the paragraph; mark corrections in erasable pen on the overhead transparency.

5. After the paragraph is correctly divided into sentences, review it one sentence at a time. Have volunteers point out errors as you come to them, and identify the necessary corrections. Encourage students to explain the reason for each correction; explain or clarify any rules that are unfamiliar.

 EMC 2727 • Daily Paragraph Editing • ©2004 by Evan-Moor Corp.

Option 2

Follow Steps 1–4 on page 4, and then work with students to focus on one type of error at a time, correcting all errors of the same type (i.e., capitalization, commas, subject/verb agreement, spelling, etc.) in the paragraph before moving on to another type. Refer to the Error Summary in the Editing Key to help you identify the various types of errors.

Option 3

Use directed group lesson time to conduct a minilesson on one or more of the skills emphasized in that day's lesson. This is especially appropriate for new or unfamiliar skills, or for skills that are especially challenging or confusing for students. After introducing a specific skill, use the approach outlined in Option 2 to focus on that skill in one or more of the week's daily paragraphs. To provide additional practice, refer to the Skills Scope & Sequence to find other paragraphs that include the same target skill.

Individual Practice

Once students are familiar with the process for editing the daily paragraphs, they may work on their own or with a partner to make corrections. Be sure students have their Proofreading Marks (see page 10) available to help them mark their corrections. Remind students to refer to the student Language Handbook as needed for guidance in the rules of mechanics and usage. Some students may find it helpful to know at the outset the number and types of errors they are seeking. Provide this information by referring to the Error Summary on the annotated Editing Key pages. You may wish to use a transparency on the overhead to check work with the group. Occasionally, you may wish to assess students' acquisition of skills by collecting and reviewing their work before they check it.

Customizing Instruction

Some of the skills covered in *Daily Paragraph Editing* may not be part of the grade-level expectancies in the language program you use. Some skills may even be taught differently in your program from the way they are modeled in *Daily Paragraph Editing*. In such cases, follow the approach used in your program. Simply revise the paragraph text as needed by covering it with correction fluid or by writing in changes before you reproduce copies for students.

Comma usage is an area where discrepancies are most likely to arise. *Daily Paragraph Editing* uses the "closed" style, where commas are included after short introductory phrases. Except for commas used in salutations, closings, dates, and between city and state in letters, journals, or news articles, all commas that appear in the daily paragraphs have been correctly placed according to the closed style. All other skills related to the use of commas are practiced by requiring students to insert missing commas, rather than moving or deleting extraneous commas.

Occasionally, you or your students may make a correction that differs from that shown in the Editing Key. The decision to use an exclamation mark instead of a period, or a period instead of a semicolon, is often a subjective decision made by individual writers. When discrepancies of this sort arise, capitalize on the "teachable moment" to let students know that there are gray areas in English usage and mechanics, and discuss how each of the possible correct choices can affect the meaning or tone of the writing.

You may wish to have your students mark corrections on the daily paragraphs in a manner that differs from the common proofreading marks on page 10. If so, model the marking style you wish students to follow as you conduct group lessons on an overhead, and point out any differences between the standard proofing marks and those to be used by your students.

Using the Writing Prompts

Have students keep their daily paragraphs in a folder so they can review the week's four corrected paragraphs on Friday. Identify the type of writing modeled in the four-paragraph composition and any of its special features (e.g., dialog in a fictional narrative; salutation, closing, and paragraph style in a letter; opinion statements and supporting arguments in an editorial; etc.).

Present the Friday writing prompt on an overhead transparency, write it on the board, or distribute individual copies to students. Take a few minutes to brainstorm ideas with the group and to focus on language skills that students will need to address in their writing.

After students complete their writing, encourage them to use the Editing Checklist (see page 11) to review or revise their work. You may also wish to have partners review each other's writing. To conduct a more formal assessment of students' writing, use the Assessment Rubric on page 9.

If you assign paragraph writing for homework, be sure students have the week's four corrected paragraphs available as a reference. You may wish to set aside some time for volunteers to read their completed writing to the class, or display compositions on a weekly writing bulletin board for students to enjoy.

EMC 2727 • Daily Paragraph Editing • ©2004 by Evan-Moor Corp.

Skills Scope and Sequence

Week No.

Capitalization	1	2	3	4	5	6	7	8	9	10	11	12	13	14	15	16	17	18	19	20	21	22	23	24	25	26	27	28	29	30	31	32	33	34	35	36
Beginning of Sentences, Quotations, Salutations/Closings	●	●	●	●	●	●	●	●	●	●	●	●	●	●	●	●	●	●	●	●	●	●	●	●	●	●	●	●	●	●	●	●	●	●	●	●
Days & Months					●					●	●			●				●								●				●	●	●	●	●		
Incorrect Use of Capitals			●		●	●			●		●		●	●			●		●				●	●	●			●	●	●		●		●	●	
Names & Titles of People, incl. Languages, Nationalities	●			●	●	●			●	●	●		●			●	●		●	●		●	●		●				●			●	●	●	●	●
Names of Places, Historical Events, Specific Things	●			●	●				●		●		●				●	●		●			●						●			●	●			
Nouns Used as Names (Aunt, Grandpa, etc.)							●					●								●			●		●			●	●		●					
Titles of Books, Magazines, Poems, Stories				●																●			●		●				●							
Names of Ships, Aircraft, Space Vehicles										●													●								●					
Word I				●		●									●				●										●		●		●			

Language Usage	1	2	3	4	5	6	7	8	9	10	11	12	13	14	15	16	17	18	19	20	21	22	23	24	25	26	27	28	29	30	31	32	33	34	35	36
Correct Use of Singular & Plural Forms	●		●		●	●	●			●	●	●	●	●	●	●			●	●	●	●	●	●	●	●	●	●	●	●		●		●	●	●
Correct Use of Verb Tenses	●	●	●			●	●		●		●	●	●				●		●				●	●		●				●		●		●	●	●
Use of Correct Adjective & Adverbial Forms													●	●		●		●					●	●										●		●
Use of Correct Pronouns						●		●											●												●	●				

Punctuation: Apostrophes	1	2	3	4	5	6	7	8	9	10	11	12	13	14	15	16	17	18	19	20	21	22	23	24	25	26	27	28	29	30	31	32	33	34	35	36
In Contractions	●		●	●	●	●	●	●	●	●	●	●		●	●	●	●	●	●	●	●	●	●	●	●	●	●	●	●	●	●	●	●		●	●
In Possessives	●		●	●	●		●		●	●	●		●												●	●	●	●		●		●		●		●
Improperly Placed			●						●																		●									

Punctuation: Commas	1	2	3	4	5	6	7	8	9	10	11	12	13	14	15	16	17	18	19	20	21	22	23	24	25	26	27	28	29	30	31	32	33	34	35	36
After Introductory Dependent Phrase or Clause	●	●	●	●						●	●	●	●	●	●	●	●	●	●	●	●	●	●	●	●					●		●		●		●
After Introductory Interjection or Expression						●																								●						
After Salutation & Closing in a Letter				●	●																															
Between City & State & City & Country Names									●						●								●													
Between Equally Modifying Adjectives																														●	●	●				●
Between Items in a Series	●	●			●	●	●			●	●		●	●	●	●	●	●	●	●	●	●	●	●	●	●	●	●	●	●	●	●	●	●	●	●
In a Date																									●											
To Separate Parts of Compound Sentences			●	●						●				●			●						●		●					●	●		●	●	●	●
To Set Off Appositives						●	●			●	●											●			●		●				●			●		●
To Set Off Interruptions																						●	●				●					●				
To Set Off Quotations									●														●													
With Name Used in Direct Address																					●							●	●						●	

Skills Scope and Sequence (continued)

	Week No.																																			
	1	2	3	4	5	6	7	8	9	10	11	12	13	14	15	16	17	18	19	20	21	22	23	24	25	26	27	28	29	30	31	32	33	34	35	36
Punctuation: Periods																																				
After Initials	•			•																					•											
At End of Sentence	•	•	•	•	•	•	•	•	•	•	•	•	•	•	•	•	•	•	•	•	•	•	•	•	•	•	•	•	•	•	•	•	•	•	•	•
In Abbreviations (Months, Time, Measurement)					•																									•				•		•
In Title Abbreviations						•																	•							•				•		
To Correct Run-on & Rambling Sentences; Fragments			•							•		•		•		•								•			•		•				•		•	•
Punctuation: Quotation Marks																																				
In Speech										•											•							•		•		•				
To Set Apart Special Words																•											•									
With Titles of Works of Art, Articles, Poems, Chapters, Short Stories, Songs, Newspaper Articles																																	•			
Punctuation: Other																																				
Colon in Time	•																																			
Exclamation Point					•											•		•	•																	
Hyphen in Fractions																																•			•	
Periods & Commas Inside Quotation Marks															•						•															
Question Mark			•					•					•	•		•	•		•			•							•		•		•			•
Underline Names of Aircraft & Ships										•																•										
Underline Titles of Books, Magazines, Movies, Newspapers, TV Shows				•															•										•				•			
Spelling																																				
Identify Errors in Grade-Level Words	•	•	•	•	•	•	•	•	•	•	•	•	•	•	•	•	•	•	•	•	•	•	•	•	•	•	•	•	•	•	•	•	•	•	•	•

EMC 2727 • Daily Paragraph Editing • ©2004 by Evan-Moor Corp.

Assessment Rubric for Evaluating Friday Paragraph Writing

The Friday writing prompts give students the opportunity to use the capitalization, punctuation, and other usage and mechanics skills that have been practiced during the week's editing tasks. They also require students to write in a variety of different forms and genres.

In evaluating students' Friday paragraphs, you may wish to focus exclusively on their mastery of the aspects of mechanics and usage targeted that week. However, if you wish to conduct a more global assessment of student writing, the following rubric offers broad guidelines for evaluating the composition as a whole.

Characteristics of Student Writing

	EXCELLENT	GOOD	FAIR	WEAK
Clarity and Focus	Writing is exceptionally clear, focused, and interesting.	Writing is generally clear, focused, and interesting.	Writing is loosely focused on the topic.	Writing is unclear and unfocused.
Development of Main Ideas	Main ideas are clear, specific, and well-developed.	Main ideas are identifiable, but may be somewhat general.	Main ideas are overly broad or simplistic.	Main ideas are unclear or not expressed.
Organization	Organization is clear (beginning, middle, and end) and fits the topic and writing form.	Organization is clear, but may be predictable or formulaic.	Organization is attempted, but is often unclear.	Organization is not coherent.
Use of Details	Details are relevant, specific, and well-placed.	Details are relevant, but may be overly general.	Details may be off-topic, predictable, or not specific enough.	Details are absent or insufficient to support main ideas.
Vocabulary	Vocabulary is exceptionally rich, varied, and well-chosen.	Vocabulary is colorful and generally avoids clichés.	Vocabulary is ordinary and may rely on clichés.	Vocabulary is limited, general, or vague.
Mechanics and Usage	Demonstrates exceptionally strong command of conventions of punctuation, capitalization, spelling, and usage.	Demonstrates control of conventions of punctuation, capitalization, spelling, and usage.	Errors in use of conventions of mechanics and usage distract, but do not impede, the reader.	Limited ability to control conventions of mechanics and usage impairs readability of the composition.

Proofreading Marks

Use these marks to show corrections.

Mark	Meaning	Example
ℒ	Take this out (delete).	I love ~~to~~ to read.
⊙	Add a period.	It was late⊙
≡	Make this a capital letter.	First prize went to <u>m</u>aria.
/	Make this a lowercase letter.	We saw a /Black /Cat.
——	Fix the spelling.	This is our ~~hause~~ house.
⌄	Add a comma.	Goodnight⌄Mom.
⌄	Add an apostrophe.	That⌄s Lil⌄s bike.
⌄⌄	Add quotation marks.	⌄Come in,⌄ he said.
!⌄ ?⌄	Add an exclamation point or a question mark.	Help! Can you help me?
⌃̄	Add a hyphen.	I've read three‑fourths of the book.
⌒	Close the space.	Foot⌒ball is fun.
⌃	Add a word.	The ⌃red pen is mine.
——	Underline the words.	We read <u>Old Yeller</u>.
⌃̇	Add a colon.	Alex arrived at 4⌃00.

EMC 2727 • Daily Paragraph Editing • ©2004 by Evan-Moor Corp.

Editing Checklist

Use this checklist to review and revise your writing:

- ◯ Does each sentence begin with a capital letter?

- ◯ Do names of people and places begin with a capital letter?

- ◯ Does each sentence end with a period, a question mark, or an exclamation point?

- ◯ Did I use apostrophes to show possession (*Ana's desk*) and in contractions (*isn't*)?

- ◯ Did I choose the correct word (*to, too, two*)?

- ◯ Did I check for spelling errors?

- ◯ Did I place commas where they are needed?

- ◯ Are my sentences clear and complete?

Editing Checklist

Use this checklist to review and revise your writing:

- ◯ Does each sentence begin with a capital letter?

- ◯ Do names of people and places begin with a capital letter?

- ◯ Does each sentence end with a period, a question mark, or an exclamation point?

- ◯ Did I use apostrophes to show possession (*Ana's desk*) and in contractions (*isn't*)?

- ◯ Did I choose the correct word (*to, too, two*)?

- ◯ Did I check for spelling errors?

- ◯ Did I place commas where they are needed?

- ◯ Are my sentences clear and complete?

Preview the 4 daily lessons to ensure you review or introduce skills that may be unfamiliar to students.

Kites—Not Just for Fun

People the world over ~~has~~ [have] been flying kites for centuries in fact, kites were invented over two thousand years ago! one ancient story tells of a chinese general his army was trying to overthrow a cruel emperor. the general made a kite he tied a ~~not~~ [knot] in the string Next, his soldiers flew it in the direction of the palace When the kite was over the palace the general marked the string and reeled in the kite

Error Summary	
Capitalization	6
Language Usage	1
Punctuation:	
Comma	1
Period	6
Spelling	1

MONDAY   **WEEK 1**

the general measured the length between the knot and the mark he made on the kite string.
he used this ~~mesurement~~ [measurement] to plan a tunnel to the emperors palace His soldiers spent days digging the tunnel. Finally, it was ready His soldiers crept through the tunnel they came out inside the walls of the palace The cruel emperor was ~~defeeted~~ [defeated] with the help of a simple kite!

Error Summary	
Capitalization	3
Punctuation:	
Apostrophe	1
Period	4
Spelling	2

TUESDAY   **WEEK 1**

Kites—Not Just for Fun

People the world over has been flying kites for centuries in fact, kites were invented over two thousand years ago! one ancient story tells of a chinese general his army was trying to overthrow a cruel emperor. the general made a kite he tied a not in the string Next, his soldiers flew it in the direction of the palace When the kite was over the palace the general marked the string and reeled in the kite

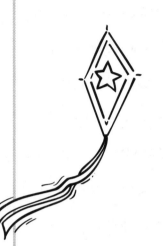

WATCH FOR

• run-on sentences

MONDAY   **WEEK 1**

the general measured the length between the knot and the mark he made on the kite string. he used this mesurement to plan a tunnel to the emperors palace His soldiers spent days digging the tunnel. Finally, it was ready His soldiers crept through the tunnel they came out inside the walls of the palace The cruel emperor was defeeted with the help of a simple kite!

WATCH FOR

• run-on sentences

TUESDAY   **WEEK 1**

            have

Kites ~~has~~ also been used in modern warfare. before airplanes were invented cameras were tied to kites they were sent high in the air to take pictures. This was a way of gathering information about ~~enemi~~ enemy forces. kites have also been used to carry radio equipment up into the air this made it easier to send and ~~recieve~~ receive signals. Kites were used in emergency lifeboat kits to help lost boats signal to searchers

Error Summary

Capitalization	4
Language Usage	1
Punctuation:	
Comma	1
Period	3
Spelling	2

WEDNESDAY   **WEEK 1**

Even though kites have been used for warfare they are mainly used for fun. People fly kites at parks and beaches. Some places hold yearly kite-flying contests or festivals. In both china and japan special holidays include kite-flying as part of the celebration. kites can be large and expensive or simple and affordable. You can easily make a kite by using sticks paper tape and string. So go fly a kite!

Error Summary

Capitalization	3
Punctuation:	
Comma	5
Other	1

THURSDAY   **WEEK 1**

Name _____

Kites has also been used in modern warfare. before airplanes were invented cameras were tied to kites they were sent high in the air to take pictures. This was a way of gathering information about enemi forces. kites have also been used to carry radio equipment up into the air this made it easier to send and recieve signals. Kites were used in emergency lifeboat kits to help lost boats signal to searchers

• run-on sentences

WEDNESDAY   **WEEK 1**

Even though kites have been used for warfare they are mainly used for fun. People fly kites at parks and beaches. Some places hold yearly kite-flying contests or festivals. In both china and japan special holidays include kite-flying as part of the celebration. kites can be large and expensive or simple and affordable. You can easily make a kite by using sticks paper tape and string. So go fly a kite

• commas

• exclamation points

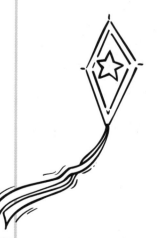

THURSDAY   **WEEK 1**

How Traits Travel

Do you think that plants could help scientists learn about people? Although it may seem odd gregor mendel found that he could learn a lot about people by studying plants. actually, plants helped Mendel learn about heredity heredity is the way traits pass from parents to children In humans, eye color hair color skin color and height are all traits. They are ~~past~~ passed on ~~threw~~ through heredity.

Error Summary

Capitalization	4
Punctuation:	
Comma	4
Period	2
Other	1
Spelling	2

MONDAY   **WEEK 2**

Gregor mendel was born into a farming family in 1823 he was a gifted student. His family could not afford to pay for university studies Instead, mendel became a monk at the time, this was a good way for mendel to keep studying and learning. He also began to teach science to high school students Mendel loved nature. He ~~love~~ loved to walk in the garden among the plants. on one of these walks mendel saw an unusual plant. he ~~decide~~ decided to study it.

Error Summary

Capitalization	8
Language Usage	2
Punctuation:	
Comma	1
Period	4

TUESDAY   **WEEK 2**

Name _____

How Traits Travel

Do you think that plants could help scientists learn about people. Although it may seem odd gregor mendel found that he could learn a lot about people by studying plants. actually, plants helped Mendel learn about heredity heredity is the way traits pass from parents to children In humans, eye color hair color skin color and height are all traits. They are past on threw heredity.

• commas

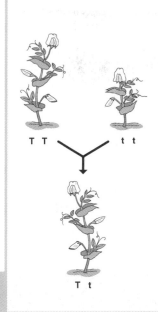

MONDAY   **WEEK 2**

Gregor mendel was born into a farming family in 1823 he was a gifted student. His family could not afford to pay for university studies Instead, mendel became a monk at the time, this was a good way for mendel to keep studying and learning. He also began to teach science to high school students Mendel loved nature. He love to walk in the garden among the plants. on one of these walks mendel saw an unusual plant. he decide to study it.

• commas

TUESDAY   **WEEK 2**

Mendel planted the unusual plant next to a common type of plant. He wanted to see if plants that grew in the same conditions would look alike when new plants grew mendel saw that they did not look alike. Each new plant looked like the "parent" plant that it ~~come~~ came from. Mendel wondered about this? He wondered if new plants always looked like the parent plants Mendel planned more ~~studys~~ studies.

Error Summary

Capitalization	2
Language Usage	1
Punctuation:	
Comma	1
Period	3
Spelling	1

WEDNESDAY   **WEEK 2**

Mendel ~~growed~~ grew plants from two tall parent plants. He ~~growed~~ grew plants from two short parent plants. He also ~~grew~~ grew plants with one tall and one short parent. When both parent plants were alike the new plants looked like the parents. The plant that grew from a tall and a short parent was tall mendel later learned that some traits are stronger than others his discoveries helped us learn how human traits are passed from parents to children.

Error Summary

Capitalization	2
Language Usage	3
Punctuation:	
Comma	1
Period	2

THURSDAY   **WEEK 2**

Mendel planted the unusual plant next to a common type of plant. He wanted to see if plants that grew in the same conditions would look alike when new plants grew mendel saw that they did not look alike. Each new plant looked like the "parent" plant that it come from. Mendel wondered about this? He wondered if new plants always looked like the parent plants Mendel planned more studys.

• commas

WEDNESDAY   **WEEK 2**

Mendel growed plants from two tall parent plants. He growed plants from two short parent plants. He also grow plants with one tall and one short parent. When both parent plants were alike the new plants looked like the parents. The plant that grew from a tall and a short parent was tall mendel later learned that some traits are stronger than others his discoveries helped us learn how human traits are passed from parents to children.

• commas

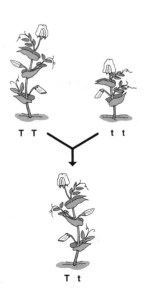

THURSDAY   **WEEK 2**

Preview the 4 daily lessons to ensure you review or introduce skills that may be unfamiliar to students.

Uniforms Are Not the Answer

It seems that more and more schools these days are choosing to have student's wear uniforms At first, school officials reasons seem to make a lot of ~~cents~~ sense Those who support school uniforms ~~beleive~~ believe that switching over to uniforms can help schools solve many problems. it would be wonderful if tough problems could be solved with such easy answers. Its ~~to~~ too bad that is just not the case.

Error Summary

Capitalization	1
Punctuation:	
Apostrophe	2
Period	2
Spelling	4

MONDAY   **WEEK 3**

Those who support uniforms say that they will help make all students equal They also believes that students will focus on schoolwork instead of comparing ~~there~~ their classmates clothes Uniform supporters feel that shopping for clothing will be ~~easyer~~ easier For student's and parents a like some say that uniforms may even help solve the gang problems that some schools are facing

Error Summary

Capitalization	2
Language Usage	2
Punctuation:	
Apostrophe	1
Period	5
Spelling	4

TUESDAY   **WEEK 3**

Name

Uniforms Are Not the Answer

It seems that more and more schools these days are choosing to have student's wear uniforms At first, school officials reasons seem to make a lot of cents Those who support school uniforms beleive that switching over to uniforms can help schools solve many problems. it would be wonderful if tough problems could be solved with such easy answers. Its to bad that is just not the case.

• apostrophes

MONDAY	WEEK 3

Those who support uniforms say that they will help make all students equal They also believes that students will focus on schoolwork instead of comparing there classmates clothes Uniform supporters feel that shopping for clothing will be easier. For student's and parents a like some say that uniforms may even help solve the gang problems that some schools facing

• apostrophes

TUESDAY	WEEK 3

This kind of thinking just doesnt make sense
Kids who join gangs will not change. Just because
they wear uniforms at school. it may seem easier to
let the school decide what students wear each day
but is it really a good idea in the long run? The job
of parents and teachers is to help children learn to
make good choices. Dont kids deserve to practice
making good choices every chance they get?

Error Summary

Capitalization	2
Punctuation:	
Apostrophe	2
Comma	1
Period	2
Other	2
Spelling	2

WEDNESDAY　　　　　　　　　WEEK 3

If we want kids to think for themselves when
they grow up we need to let them make simple
decisions as soon as they are ready. Choosing clothes
for school is an easy way to practice making good
choices. Adults should help children learn. To make
good decisions and to think for themselves. We
should be sure that there are caring adults at
home and at school to help guide every child

Error Summary

Capitalization	1
Language Usage	2
Punctuation:	
Comma	1
Period	2
Spelling	1

THURSDAY　　　　　　　　　WEEK 3

This kind of thinking just doesnt make sense Kids who join gangs will not change. Just because they wear uniforms at school. it may seem easier to let the school deside what students ware each day but is it really a good idea in the long run. The job of parents and teachers is to help children learn to make good choices. Dont kids deserve to practice making good choices every chance they get.

• apostrophes

WEDNESDAY   **WEEK 3**

If we want kids to think for themselves when they grow up we need to let them make simple decisions as soon as they is ready. Choosing clothes for school is an easy way to practice making good choices. Adults should help children learn. To make good decisions and to think for themselves. We should be shure that there are caring adults at home and at school to help guide every children

THURSDAY   **WEEK 3**

Preview the 4 daily lessons to ensure you review or introduce skills that may be unfamiliar to students.

Pen Pals

dear Ana

    I was so happy to get your letter last week. Now that school has started again, it seems like ages ago that we were at summer camp. Im glad that were keeping our promise to stay in touch!

    Forth [Fourth] grade has been fun so far, i am still taking violin lessons, and i'm also playing on a basketball team after school. dad doesnt want me to get to [too] busy because we get homework every day now

Error Summary	
Capitalization	4
Punctuation:	
Apostrophe	3
Comma	3
Period	2
Spelling	2

MONDAY   **WEEK 4**

    What have you been reading these days? we are reading island of the blue dolphins. So far, i really like it. We are learning about the Native americans of california, and my teacher makes it lots of fun. today we collected acorns to make acorn meel [meal].

    Please write soon and tell me all about what you are doing.

    your friend,

    Mayra

Error Summary	
Capitalization	9
Punctuation:	
Comma	2
Period	2
Other	1
Spelling	1

TUESDAY   **WEEK 4**

Name _____

Pen Pals

dear Ana

I was so happy to get your letter last week. Now that school has started again it seems like ages ago that we were at summer camp. Im glad that were keeping our promise to stay in touch!

Forth grade has been fun so far i am still taking violin lessons and i'm also playing on a basketball team after school. dad doesnt want me to get to busy because we get homework every day now

MONDAY	WEEK 4

What have you been reading these days we are reading <u>island of the blue dolphins</u>. So far, i really like it We are learning about the Native americans of california and my teacher makes it lots of fun. today we collected acorns to make acorn meel

Please write soon and tell me all about what you are doing.

your friend

Mayra

TUESDAY	WEEK 4

dear mayra

thanks for writing back to me so quickly! I love getting letters in the mail more than getting e-mail i dont know why but i think its more exciting to find a ~~reel~~ real envelope waiting for me.

i had a good day at school today we have been ~~studyng~~ studying fractions and today we had a fraction party. My group had to divide two pizzas into equal parts for the whole class We used sixteenths.

Error Summary	
Capitalization	7
Punctuation:	
Apostrophe	2
Comma	3
Period	3
Spelling	2

WEDNESDAY   **WEEK 4**

I have been really busy with my music. i have been practicing a duet with my friend lin. Its starting ~~too~~ to sound really good. I'll bring the music to camp next summer and you and I can play it together

We've been reading By the shores of Silver lake. Weren't you reading that over the summer? I love it please write ~~agen~~ again soon

your friend

ana

Error Summary	
Capitalization	7
Punctuation:	
Apostrophe	1
Comma	2
Period	3
Other	2
Spelling	2

THURSDAY   **WEEK 4**

dear mayra

thanks for writing back to me so quickly! I love getting letters in the mail more than getting e-mail i dont know why but i think its more exciting to find a reel envelope waiting for me.

i had a good day at school today we have been studyng fractions and today we had a fraction party. My group had to divide two pizzas into equal parts for the whole class We used sixteenths.

• letter (salutation)

WEDNESDAY　　　　　　　　　　**WEEK 4**

I have been really busy with my music. i have been practicing a duet with my friend lin. Its starting too sound really good. I'll bring the music to camp next summer and you and I can play it together

We've been reading By the shores of Silver lake. Weren't you reading that over the summer. I love it please write agen soon

your friend

ana

• letter (closing)
• book titles

THURSDAY　　　　　　　　　　**WEEK 4**

Preview the 4 daily lessons to ensure you review or introduce skills that may be unfamiliar to students.

Birthday Mail

dear daniel

you are invited to celebrate my 11th birthday with my family and me. We will be camping overnight at bat cave camp in Smoky ridge state park. We'll hike, swim, and fish at the park. We will leave at 10.00 am from my house at 9231 cypress road on saturday the 16th. your parents can pick you up at 6.00 pm at my house on sunday the 17th, or you can call them for a ride home after we get back

Error Summary	
Capitalization	14
Punctuation:	
Comma	3
Period	6
Other	2
Spelling	1

MONDAY   **WEEK 5**

We will have a tent, food, and cooking gear. You will need to bring a sleeping bag, a flashlight, extra batteries, hiking boots, a cap, insect repellent, sunscreen, and all your clothing. If you have a fishing pole, you might want to bring it along. Please call 555-3020 to let us know if you will be able to come.
I shure hope you can!

your Friend,
Nick

sure

Error Summary	
Capitalization	2
Punctuation:	
Comma	10
Period	2
Spelling	1

TUESDAY   **WEEK 5**

EMC 2727 • Daily Paragraph Editing, Grade 4 • ©2004 by Evan-Moor Corp.

Name _____

Birthday Mail

• names of places
• dates
• colons in time

dear daniel

you are invited to celebrate my 11th birthday with my family and me We will be camping overnight at bat cave camp in Smoky ridge state park. We'l hike swim and fish at the park. We will leave at 10.00 am from my house at 9231 cypress road on saturday the 16th. your parents can pick you up at 6-00 pm at my house on sunday the 17th, or you can call them for a ride home after we get back

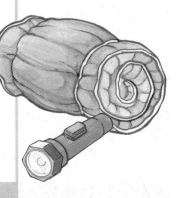

MONDAY   **WEEK 5**

We will have a tent food and cooking gear. You will need to bring a sleeping bag a flashlight extra batteries hiking boots a cap insect repellent sunscreen and all your clothing. If you have a fishing pole, you might want to bring it along? Please call 555-3020 to let us know if you will be able to come I shure hope you can!

your Friend

Nick

• commas

TUESDAY   **WEEK 5**

Dear daniel,

    thank you so much for coming to my birthday camp-out. I had a great time with Mike, Tony, and you. The headlamp you gave me was a ~~grate~~ *great* gift. it's the perfect thing to use for exploring caves. I really like having both my hands free when I'm walking in a dark cave, and a light on my head is the perfect solution. It's so much better than a regular flashlight. Thanks!

Error Summary

Capitalization	3
Punctuation:	
Apostrophe	3
Comma	2
Period	1
Other	1
Spelling	1

WEDNESDAY   **WEEK 5**

    My Mom took my film to be developed today, and the pictures from our camping trip should be ready next week. I'm not sure if the pictures we took in the cave will turn out. It might have been ~~to~~ *too* dark. i can't wait to see the pictures of that fish we caught. we are getting ~~to~~ *two* copies so that you can have some pictures for your album.

    your friend,

    nick

Error Summary

Capitalization	6
Punctuation:	
Apostrophe	1
Comma	1
Period	3
Spelling	2

THURSDAY   **WEEK 5**

Dear daniel,

thank you so much for coming to my birthday camp-out. I had a great time with Mike Tony and you. The headlamp you gave me was a grate gift its the perfect thing to use for exploring caves. I really like having both my hands free when Im walking in a dark cave, and a light on my head is the perfect solution. Its so much better than a regular flashlight. Thanks

• commas

WEDNESDAY   **WEEK 5**

My Mom took my film to be developed today, and the pictures from our camping trip should be ready next week i'm not sure if the pictures we took in the cave will turn out. It might have been to dark i cant wait to see the pictures of that fish we caught. we are getting to copies so that you can have some pictures for your album

your friend

nick

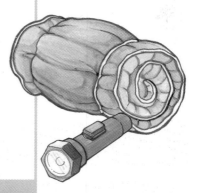

THURSDAY   **WEEK 5**

Preview the 4 daily lessons to ensure you review or introduce skills that may be unfamiliar to students.

The Letter

It was a crisp cool autumn morning and I shuffled ~~threw~~ *through* the leaves on the sidewalk. The letter carrier waved as he drove off to ~~her~~ *his* next stop i waved back and then I paused in front of the row of mailboxes. I took a deep breath exhaled slowly and opened our box. Would this be the day that the letter Id awaited so anxiously would finally come? I wasnt sure i could take even one more day of waiting

Error Summary

Capitalization	2
Language Usage	1
Punctuation:	
Apostrophe	2
Comma	5
Period	2
Other	1
Spelling	1

MONDAY   **WEEK 6**

It had been weeks since I sent my application off to space camp Id spent anxious difficult hours writing the essay that accompanied the application. my ~~sceince~~ *science* teacher Mrs uchida had ~~wrote~~ *written* me a wonderful letter of recommendation and my Mom had filled out all the required information for my scholarship request. Everything was complete so all I could do was wish hope and wait for a letter of reply.

Error Summary

Capitalization	3
Language Usage	1
Punctuation:	
Apostrophe	1
Comma	7
Period	2
Spelling	1

TUESDAY   **WEEK 6**

Name _____

The Letter

It was a crisp cool autumn morning and I shuffled threw the leaves on the sidewalk. The letter carrier waved as he drove off to her next stop i waved back and then I paused in front of the row of mailboxes. I took a deep breath exhaled slowly and opened our box. Would this be the day that the letter Id awaited so anxiously would finally come I wasnt sure i could take even one more day of waiting

- commas

MONDAY	WEEK 6

It had been weeks since I sent my application off to space camp Id spent anxious difficult hours writing the essay that accompanied the application. my sceince teacher Mrs uchida had wrote me a wonderful letter of recommendation and my Mom had filled out all the required information for my scholarship request. Everything was complete so all I could do was wish hope and wait for a letter of reply.

- commas

TUESDAY	WEEK 6

I slowly pulled open the door of the mailbox. a stack of mail was piled inside the box. Rats, the first piece was addressed to "Resident" and was just the weekly grocery ad announcing the current price of chicken, halloween candy, and seasonal fruits. below that was a letter addressed to my mom. It was from the phone company, so it was probably a bill. There was one letter left. I could hardly stand to look!

Error Summary

Capitalization	3
Punctuation:	
Comma	4
Period	2

WEDNESDAY　　　　　　　　**WEEK 6**

I took a slow, deep breath and pulled out a crisp new envelope. It was addressed to me. Yes, It was from space camp. Did the letter have good news for me, or was I about to have a terrible disappointment? I knew that plenty of other kids would be getting letters like this one. Im sure they wanted to go to space camp just as much as i did. In one more moment, I knew Id have my answer.

Error Summary

Capitalization	2
Language Usage	1
Punctuation:	
Apostrophe	2
Comma	5
Period	2
Other	1
Spelling	1

THURSDAY　　　　　　　　**WEEK 6**

I slowly pulled open the door of the mailbox a stack of mail was piled inside the box. Rats the first piece was addressed to "Resident" and was just the weekly grocery ad announcing the current price of chicken halloween candy and seasonal fruits. below that was a letter addressed to my mom. It was from the phone company so it was probably a bill. There was one letter left I could hardly stand to look!

WATCH FOR

• commas

WEDNESDAY   **WEEK 6**

I took a slow deep breath and pulled out a crisp new envelope. It was addressed to me. Yes It was from space camp Did the letter have good news for me or was I about to have a terrible disappointment. I knew that plenty of other kid would be getting letters like this one Im sure they wanted to go to space camp just as much as i did. In one more moment I new Id have my answer.

WATCH FOR

• commas

THURSDAY   **WEEK 6**

Preview the 4 daily lessons to ensure you review or introduce skills that may be unfamiliar to students.

A New Life in Old California

It has been more than five years since we left our home in New spain it seemed like we had ~~live~~ lived there forever. After all, I had ~~spended~~ spent all eight years of my life ~~their~~ there. That time and place ~~seem~~ seems so distant now. Sometimes it feels like our new home in Salinas, Alta california, is worlds away from new spain it was such a tiring, difficult journey between our old home and our new one that we might as well be in another world!

Error Summary

Capitalization	6
Language Usage	3
Punctuation:	
Comma	1
Period	3
Spelling	1

MONDAY   **WEEK 7**

Sailing ships seldom bring supplies to old california. Almost everything we have must be ~~groan~~ grown or made with our own hands. our home is a simple one made of adobe. we have far fewer comforts than we did in new spain. We all must work hard to finish the work That must be done every day. Only my youngest brother pedro, who was born here in alta California, does not have a job to do.

Error Summary

Capitalization	9
Punctuation:	
Comma	3
Period	2
Spelling	1

TUESDAY   **WEEK 7**

Name _____

A New Life in Old California

It has been more than five years since we left our home in New spain it seemed like we had live there forever. After all, I had spent all eight years of my life their. That time and place seem so distant now Sometimes it feels like our new home in Salinas, Alta california, is worlds away from new spain it was such a tiring difficult journey between our old home and our new one that we might as well be in another world!

- commas

MONDAY   **WEEK 7**

Sailing ships seldom bring supplies to old california. Almost everything we have must be groan or made with our own hands our home is a simple one made of adobe. we have far fewer comforts than we did in new spain. We all must work hard to finish the work That must be done every day. Only my youngest brother pedro who was born here in alta California does not have a job to do

- commas

TUESDAY   **WEEK 7**

my job is to care for the cattle I lead the cows out to the pasture Early in the morning in the late afternoon I herd them back into the barn. Besides helping me milk Marta spends the day caring for pedro. In the early evening pedro likes to sit in the kitchen while mama pats out tortillas for our dinner He likes to help pat the grainy salty cornmeal into flat round shapes that mama cooks on the griddle

Error Summary

Capitalization	7
Punctuation:	
Comma	5
Period	5

WEDNESDAY   **WEEK 7**

This week, it is Papas turn to guard the mission bandits have been ~~steeling~~ *stealing* cattle and horses in this area The settlers are all taking turns standing guard Papa says that i am old enough to ~~gard~~ *guard* the cattle at home. Next year, when i'm 14 papa says he will take me with him to the mission. Perhaps I will see lovable jolly Father beltran again he will be happy to ~~no~~ *know* that I still enjoy reading and writing

Error Summary

Capitalization	6
Punctuation:	
Apostrophe	1
Comma	2
Period	5
Spelling	3

THURSDAY   **WEEK 7**

Name _____

my job is to care for the cattle I lead the cows out to the pasture. Early in the morning in the late afternoon I herd them back into the barn. Besides helping me milk Marta spends the day caring for pedro. In the early evening pedro likes to sit in the kitchen while mama pats out tortillas for our dinner? He likes to help pat the grainy salty cornmeal into flat round shapes that mama cooks on the griddle

• commas

WEDNESDAY   **WEEK 7**

This week, it is Papas turn to guard the mission bandits have been steeling cattle and horses in this area The settlers are all taking turns standing guard? Papa says that i am old enough to gard the cattle at home. Next year, when i'm 14 papa says he will take me with him to the mission. Perhaps I will see lovable jolly Father beltran again he will be happy to no that I still enjoy reading and writing

• commas

THURSDAY   **WEEK 7**

Preview the 4 daily lessons to ensure you review or introduce skills that may be unfamiliar to students.

Lewis & Clark

The United states of america was a young nation in the early 1800s. It was much smaller than it is today, as it ~~reacht~~ reached only from the Atlantic Ocean to the mississippi river. In 1803, the government of the united states ~~buyed~~ bought a large area of land from france. This land was known as the "louisiana Territory." It stretched from the mississippi river to the rocky Mountains. Many native americans lived there.

Error Summary

Capitalization	13
Language Usage	1
Punctuation:	
Period	1
Spelling	1

MONDAY   **WEEK 8**

Thomas jefferson was the president who bought the louisiana territory. He had many questions about this new land. What kinds of plants, animals, and people could be found on these lands? President jefferson ~~wundered~~ wondered what the land west of the rocky mountains was like. he knew some of it was mexicos land, but he couldn't help wondering if there was a route by river that would lead to the pacific Ocean.

Error Summary

Capitalization	9
Punctuation:	
Apostrophe	1
Comma	3
Period	3
Other	1
Spelling	1

TUESDAY   **WEEK 8**

          EMC 2727 • Daily Paragraph Editing, Grade 4 • ©2004 by Evan-Moor Corp.

Name _____

Lewis & Clark

The United states of america was a young nation in the early 1800s. It was much smaller than it is today, as it reacht only from the Atlantic Ocean to the mississippi river. In 1803, the government of the united states buyed a large area of land from france. This land was known as the "louisiana Territory." It stretched from the mississippi river to the rocky Mountains. Many native americans lived there

WATCH FOR
• names of places

MONDAY   **WEEK 8**

Thomas jefferson was the president who bought the louisiana territory. He had many questions about this new land What kinds of plants animals and people could be found on these lands. President jefferson wundered what the land west of the rocky mountains was like he knew some of it was mexicos land but he couldn't help wondering if there was a route by river that would lead to the pacific Ocean

WATCH FOR
• names of places

TUESDAY   **WEEK 8**

President jefferson decided to have a group of explorers cross the new land. He wanted them to draw maps, study plants and animals, and learn about the natives. He put Captain Meriwether Lewis in charge of the explorers, and capt. lewis chose william Clark to help him lead the group. it took months to prepare for the ~~journie~~ journey. on may 14, 1804, lewis and clark set out with more than 30 explorers.

Error Summary

Capitalization	9
Punctuation:	
Comma	5
Period	1
Spelling	1

WEDNESDAY   **WEEK 8**

The explorers spent the winter of 1804 in the area now known as north dakota. There they ~~meet~~ met a french canadian trader and sacagawea, his young native american wife. both of them joined the expedition. Sacagawea helped to find food and make ~~frends~~ friends with other natives. By november of 1805, the group reached the pacific Ocean. When they returned home, they were welcomed as heroes.

Error Summary

Capitalization	10
Language Usage	1
Punctuation:	
Comma	3
Period	4
Spelling	1

THURSDAY   **WEEK 8**

EMC 2727 • *Daily Paragraph Editing, Grade 4* • ©2004 by Evan-Moor Corp.

Name _____

President jefferson decided to have a group of explorers cross the new land. He wanted them to draw maps study plants and animals and learn about the natives He put Captain Meriwether Lewis in charge of the explorers and capt. lewis chose william Clark to help him lead the group. it took months to prepare for the journie. on may 14 1804 lewis and clark set out with more than 30 explorers.

WATCH FOR

- names of people
- commas

WEDNESDAY   **WEEK 8**

The explorers spent the winter of 1804 in the area now known as north dakota. There they meet a french canadian trader and sacagawea his young native american wife both of them joined the expedition Sacagawea helped to find food and make frends with other natives By november of 1805 the group reached the pacific Ocean. When they returned home they were welcomed as heroes

WATCH FOR

- names of people
- commas

THURSDAY   **WEEK 8**

Preview the 4 daily lessons to ensure you review or introduce skills that may be unfamiliar to students.

The Everglades

The United states of america stretches from the pacific ocean to the atlantic ocean with lots of land in between Each region of the country ~~are~~ is unique? A special feature of the southeast is a wet grassy area in florida this area is called "the Everglades." The Everglades has been described as a "river of grass" Thats because currents of fresh water ~~flee~~ flow through the grass to form the Everglades special habitats.

Error Summary

Capitalization	9
Language Usage	1
Punctuation:	
Apostrophe	2
Comma	1
Period	5
Spelling	1

MONDAY   **WEEK 9**

The everglades ~~spreds~~ spreads across millions of acres it is home to thousands of species of plants and animals. Many of these plants and animals were found only in the unique varied habitats of the everglades. There ~~is~~ are many different types of habitats in the Everglades these include mangrove forests, cypress groves marine estuaries and freshwater sloughs.

Error Summary

Capitalization	4
Language Usage	1
Punctuation:	
Comma	3
Period	2
Spelling	1

TUESDAY   **WEEK 9**

Name _____

The Everglades

• names of places

The United states of america stretches from the pacific ocean to the atlantic ocean with lots of land in between Each region of the country are unique? A special feature of the southeast is a wet grassy area in florida this area is called "the Everglades." The Everglades has been described as a "river of grass" Thats because currents of fresh water floe through the grass to form the Everglades special habitats

MONDAY   **WEEK 9**

• commas

The everglades spreds across millions of acres it is home to thousands of species of plants and animals. Many of these plants and animals were found only in the unique varied habitats of the everglades. There is many different types of habitats in the Everglades these include mangrove forests, cypress groves marine estuaries and freshwater sloughs.

TUESDAY   **WEEK 9**

Each Everglades habitat needs to keep a delicate
balance to stay ~~helthy~~ [healthy]. When things get out of
balance[,] problems begin. For example, ~~kemicals~~ [chemicals] that
pollute the ~~everglades~~ can kill algae[.] algae are a simple
life-form at the bottom of the food chain. If the
algae disappear[,] the animals that eat algae ~~has~~ [have] no food[.]
this can cause plants and animals in the food chain to
~~became~~ [become] out of balance[.]

Error Summary

Capitalization	3
Language Usage	2
Punctuation:	
Comma	2
Period	3
Spelling	2

WEDNESDAY   **WEEK 9**

Today, the ~~bigest~~ [biggest] cause of problems in the
~~everglades~~ is people. People have tried to ~~drane~~ [drain] away
water so they can build homes there[.] They have also
tried to change the direction that water flows in the
~~everglades~~. These changes have created many problems
in the ~~everglade's~~ habitats. ~~Sientists~~ [Scientists] are trying to
find a way to make the ~~everglades~~ healthy again so
this unique ecosystem will be preserved[.]

Error Summary

Capitalization	4
Punctuation:	
Apostrophe	1
Period	2
Spelling	3

THURSDAY   **WEEK 9**

Each Everglades habitat needs to keep a delicate balance to stay helthy. When things get out of balance problems begin. For example, kemicals that pollute the everglades can kill algae algae are a simple life-form at the bottom of the food chain. If the algae disappear the animals that eat algae has no food this can cause plants and animals in the food chain to became out of balance

• commas

WEDNESDAY   **WEEK 9**

Today, the bigest cause of problems in the everglades is people. People have tried to drane away water so they can build homes there They have also tried to change the direction that water flows in the everglades. These changes have created many problems in the everglade's habitats. Sientists are trying to find a way to make the everglades healthy again so this unique ecosystem will be preserved

• spelling

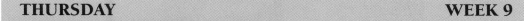

THURSDAY   **WEEK 9**

Preview the 4 daily lessons to ensure you review or introduce skills that may be unfamiliar to students.

Arrowheads in Space

What do ~~eagel~~ *eagle* feathers and arrowheads have to do with the International Space Station? american astronaut john Herrington took these items with him when he ~~ride~~ *rode* the space shuttle endeavour into outer space in november 2002. The leader of the chickasaw Nation and 200 of it's 5,000 members traveled from Oklahoma To cape Canaveral florida, to see herringtons historic launch.

Error Summary	
Capitalization	9
Language Usage	1
Punctuation:	
Apostrophe	1
Comma	2
Period	1
Other	2
Spelling	1

MONDAY   **WEEK 10**

John herrington is one-eighth chickasaw through his great-grandmother on his mothers side. Herringtons mother ~~make~~ *made* sure to register john as a member of the chickasaw tribe. When talking about his native american heritage herrington has said "I take tremendous pride in who I am and where I come from. The chickasaw nation is also very ~~prowd~~ *proud* of the first american indian in outer space.

Error Summary	
Capitalization	11
Language Usage	1
Punctuation:	
Apostrophe	2
Comma	2
Quotation Mark	1
Spelling	1

TUESDAY   **WEEK 10**

Name _____

Arrowheads in Space

What do eagel feathers and arrowheads have to do with the International Space Station american astronaut john Herrington took these items with him when he ride the space shuttle endeavour into outer space in november 2002. The leader of the chickasaw Nation and 200 of it's 5,000 members traveled from Oklahoma. To cape Canaveral florida, to see herringtons historic launch.

• names of aircraft
• names of people

MONDAY	**WEEK 10**

John herrington is one-eighth chickasaw through his great-grandmother on his mothers side. Herringtons mother make sure to register john as a member of the chickasaw tribe. When talking about his native american heritage herrington has said "I take tremendous pride in who I am and where I come from. The chickasaw nation is also very prowd of the first american indian in outer space.

• names of people

TUESDAY	**WEEK 10**

Herrington's family moved 14 times within oklahoma, colorado, wyoming, and texas during his school years. that made studying difficult. Herrington first enrolled in college to become a forest ranger, but he flunked out. Later, he returned to college and studied math and engineering. After that, herrington entered the u.s. Navy and became a test pilot. in 1996, he joined NASA to train as an astronaut.

Error Summary

Capitalization	9
Language Usage	1
Punctuation:	
Apostrophe	1
Comma	4
Period	4
Spelling	1

WEDNESDAY   **WEEK 10**

Native american artifacts were not the only items herrington carried to the space station. a special piece of equipment that cost $390 million was also on board the Endeavour. Herrington and other members of the space station crew hooked up the equipment to the orbiting station during a series of spacewalks. Spare parts were also shuttled to the space station by herrington and the Endeavour crew.

Error Summary

Capitalization	4
Punctuation:	
Period	1
Other	2
Spelling	2

THURSDAY   **WEEK 10**

Herringtons family moved 14 times within oklahoma colorado wyoming and texas during his school years that made studyng difficult. Herrington first enrolled in college to become a forest ranger but he flunked out. Later, he returned to college and study math and engineering After that, herrington entered the u.s. Navy and became a test pilot in 1996, he joined NASA to train as an astronaut

• commas

WEDNESDAY   **WEEK 10**

Native american artifacts were not the only items herrington carryed to the space station a special piece of equipment that cost $390 million was also on board the Endeavour. Herrington and other members of the space station crue hooked up the equipment to the orbiting station during a series of spacewalks. Spare parts were also shuttled to the space station by herrington and the Endeavour crew.

• names of aircraft

THURSDAY   **WEEK 10**

Preview the 4 daily lessons to ensure you review or introduce skills that may be unfamiliar to students.

A Monumental Tribute

In 1923, Doane robinson had a big idea. He
wanted
~~want~~ to carve a huge sculpture into the granite
rock of south dakota, his home state. He wanted
to honor people who helped to make the united
states a great nation He wanted to honor native
               leaders
american ~~leeders~~ such as Chief crazy horse, a Sioux
leader. He also wanted to honor american explorers
like lewis and Clark.

Error Summary

Capitalization	11
Language Usage	1
Punctuation:	
Comma	1
Period	2
Spelling	1

MONDAY   **WEEK 11**

In 1924, robinson hired Gutzon borglum, a
sculptor, to create the enormous carving together,
borglum and robinson chose mount Rushmore as
the place for the monument. mount rushmore is in
                    has
south dakota, and it ~~have~~ tall granite cliffs. Borglum
                            country's
proposed that the carving show the ~~countrie's~~ most
famous presidents. Robinson agreed that more people
would probably come to see famous presidents.

Error Summary

Capitalization	10
Language Usage	1
Punctuation:	
Comma	3
Period	3
Spelling	1

TUESDAY   **WEEK 11**

Name _____

A Monumental Tribute

In 1923, Doane robinson had a big idea. He want to carve a huge sculpture into the granite rock of south dakota, his home state. He wanted to honor people who helped to make the united states a great nation He wanted to honor native american leeders such as Chief crazy horse a Sioux leader. He also wanted to honor american explorers like lewis and Clark

- names of people
- names of places

MONDAY   **WEEK 11**

In 1924, robinson hired Gutzon borglum a sculptor to create the enormous carving together, borglum and robinson chose mount Rushmore as the place for the monument mount rushmore is in south dakota and it have tall granite cliffs. Borglum proposed that the carving show the countrie's most famous presidents. Robinson agreed that more people would probably come to see famous presidents

- commas

TUESDAY   **WEEK 11**

Plans and models for the project had been completed by 1927. For 14 years, workers continued to blast, drill, and hammer away at the rock. the faces of george washington, thomas jefferson, theodore roosevelt, and abraham lincoln all began to take shape. On october 31, 1941, the mount rushmore National Memorial was completed. Seven years later, work on another rock sculpture began.

Error Summary

Capitalization	12
Punctuation:	
Comma	7
Period	2

WEDNESDAY   **WEEK 11**

In 1948, a sioux leader, chief henry standing Bear, began to work on a memorial to honor the Sioux Nation. this sculpture would show chief crazy horse, a leeder (leader) and warrior who protected the sioux lands from the u.s. Army. Work on the crazy horse memorial is still gone (going) on today. When it is completed, it will be the worlds largest sculpture. The crazy Horse Memorial will be 87 foot (feet) tall!

Error Summary

Capitalization	16
Language Usage	2
Punctuation:	
Apostrophe	1
Comma	3
Period	1
Spelling	1

THURSDAY   **WEEK 11**

Plans and models for the project had been completed by 1927. For 14 years, workers continued to blast drill and hammer away at the rock the faces of george washington thomas jefferson theodore roosevelt and abraham lincoln all began to take shape. On october 31 1941 the mount rushmore National Memorial was completed. Seven years later, work on another rock sculpture began

- commas
- names of people

WEDNESDAY   **WEEK 11**

In 1948, A sioux leader, chief henry standing Bear began to work on a memorial to honor the Sioux Nation this sculpture would show chief crazy horse a leeder and warrior who protected the sioux lands from the u.s. Army. Work on the crazy horse memorial is still gone on today. When it is completed it will be the worlds largest sculpture. The crazy Horse Memorial will be 87 foot tall!

- commas
- names of people

THURSDAY   **WEEK 11**

Preview the 4 daily lessons to ensure you review or introduce skills that may be unfamiliar to students.

My Tree House

When I need a ~~quite~~ *quiet* place to sit and think i have just the perfect place to go and be by myself. Its not far from my home but it feels like I'm in another world when I go there. Its through the gate in the back fence across the empty lot and right at the edge of the field. That's where my tree grows and thats where I can climb up into the branches and into a world of my very own.

Error Summary

Capitalization	1
Punctuation:	
Apostrophe	3
Comma	5
Spelling	1

MONDAY   **WEEK 12**

The first day we came to see this house my Dad let me ~~warnder~~ *wander* through the backyard while he looked inside. The boy who was moving out of the house ~~come~~ *came* out into the yard. Without saying a word he opened the back gate. in silence, he led me ~~accross~~ *across* the empty lot to a tree. As he started to climb he looked down To be sure i had ~~find~~ *found* the first foothold. I was right behind him

Error Summary

Capitalization	4
Language Usage	2
Punctuation:	
Comma	3
Period	2
Spelling	3

TUESDAY   **WEEK 12**

Name _____

My Tree House

When I need a quite place to sit and think i have just the perfect place to go and be by myself. Its not far from my home but it feels like I'm in another world when I go there. Its through the gate in the back fence across the empty lot and right at the edge of the field. That's where my tree grows and thats where I can climb up into the branches and into a world of my very own.

- commas
- apostrophes

MONDAY   **WEEK 12**

The first day we came to see this house my Dad let me warnder through the backyard while he looked inside. The boy who was moving out of the house come out into the yard. Without saying a word he opened the back gate. in silence, he led me accross the empty lot to a tree. As he started to climb he looked down. To be sure i had find the first foothold. I was right be hind him

- commas

TUESDAY   **WEEK 12**

Maybe it was because the boy showed me the tree house without saying a word, maybe it was because i felt he had shared a special secret ~~seacret~~ with me. Im not sure. Ive never said a word about the tree house to anyone, but dad probably knows about it. He's seen me disappear ~~disapear~~ out the back gate countless times. you can even see a corner of the tree house from our driveway ~~drivewaye~~.

Error Summary

Capitalization	4
Punctuation:	
Apostrophe	2
Comma	1
Period	3
Spelling	4

WEDNESDAY   **WEEK 12**

I guess dad understands ~~understand~~ that the tree house is a special place for me. Its a place for me to be alone. I love to lie on my back and stare up at the green leaves ~~leafs~~ against the blue sky i love to take a book and get lost for hours in a world of adventure. Maybe what i love best of all is that this special place is mine, and I dont have to share it with anybody else. its a place all my own ~~owne~~.

Error Summary

Capitalization	4
Language Usage	1
Punctuation:	
Apostrophe	3
Comma	1
Period	2
Spelling	4

THURSDAY   **WEEK 12**

EMC 2727 • Daily Paragraph Editing, Grade 4 • ©2004 by Evan-Moor Corp.

Name _____

Maybe it was because the boy showed me the tree house without saying a word may be it was because i felt he had shared a special seacret with me. Im not sure. Ive never said a word about the tree house to anyone but dad probably knows about it. He's seen me disapear out the back gate countless times. you can even see a corner of the tree house. from our drivewaye

- spelling

WEDNESDAY   **WEEK 12**

I guess dad understand that the tree house is a special place for me. Its a place for me to be a lone. I love to lie on my back and stare up at the green leafs against the blue sky i love to take a book and get lost for hours in a world of adventure. May be what i love best of all is that this special place is mine and I dont have to share it with anybody else its a place all my owne.

- spelling

THURSDAY   **WEEK 12**

Preview the 4 daily lessons to ensure you review or introduce skills that may be unfamiliar to students.

Gold!

In 1848, there were about 20,000 ~~peepil~~ *people* living in California. Just four years later that number ~~grow~~ *grew* to over 200,000. Why did so many people come to california? they came for the Gold Rush! The Gold rush began in 1849 when a man named james marshall found a gold nugget in the american River He could not keep this ~~ekciting~~ *exciting* news to himself. In about six weeks almost every man in california was panning for gold.

Error Summary	
Capitalization	7
Language Usage	1
Punctuation:	
Comma	2
Period	1
Other	1
Spelling	2

MONDAY   **WEEK 13**

when word of james marshalls discovery reached the newspapers working men across the united states quickly ~~loded~~ *loaded* up their wagons or boarded ships and headed to California. Dreams of striking it rich ~~keeped~~ *kept* the men hopeful during the harsh difficult journey. why were these men called "forty-niners"? They got that nickname because they headed for the gold country in the year 1849

Error Summary	
Capitalization	6
Language Usage	1
Punctuation:	
Apostrophe	1
Comma	2
Period	1
Other	1
Spelling	1

TUESDAY   **WEEK 13**

Name _____

Gold!

In 1848, there were about 20,000 peepil living in California. Just four years later that number grow to over 200,000. Why did so many people come to california. they came for the Gold Rush! The Gold rush began in 1849 when a man named james marshall found a gold nugget in the american River He could not keep this ekciting news to himself. In about six weeks almost every man in california was panning for gold.

WATCH FOR

• question marks

MONDAY   **WEEK 13**

when word of james marshalls discovery reached the newspapers working men across the united states quickly loded up their wagons or boarded ships and headed to California. Dreams of striking it rich keeped the men hopeful during the harsh difficult journey. why were these men called "forty-niners" They got that nickname because they headed for the gold country in the year 1849

WATCH FOR

• question marks

TUESDAY   **WEEK 13**

To begin mining for gold men had to find some land that had not yet been claimed. Most miners claimed land along rivers and streams. Although much of this land belong (belonged) to native americans that did not stop the eager greedy gold miners from claiming it for themselves. Once a miner made a claim he began to pan for gold. What is panning for gold? It is a simple method for separating gold from sand.

Error Summary	
Capitalization	2
Language Usage	1
Punctuation:	
Comma	4
Period	3
Other	1

WEDNESDAY　　　　　　　　**WEEK 13**

By the late 1850s most of the surface gold in the rivers and streams (streems) was gone. some of the forty-niners went to work for large mining companies. others give (gave) up mining for gold and they looked for work on ranches or in stores. Few miners actually struck it rich. The gold Rush was over as quickly as it began but it had a lasting effect on the growth of california. Do you think it was a positive effect?

Error Summary	
Capitalization	4
Language Usage	1
Punctuation:	
Comma	3
Period	1
Other	1
Spelling	1

THURSDAY　　　　　　　　**WEEK 13**

To begin mining for gold men had to find some land that had not yet been claimed. Most miners claimed land along rivers and streams Although much of this land belong to native americans that did not stop the eager greedy gold miners from claiming it for themselves Once a miner made a claim he began to pan for gold What is panning for gold It is a simple method for separating gold from sand.

• question marks

WEDNESDAY   **WEEK 13**

By the late 1850s most of the surface gold in the rivers and streems was gone. some of the forty-niners went to work for large mining companies. others give up mining for gold and they looked for work on ranches or in stores Few miners actually struck it rich. The gold Rush was over as quickly as it began but it had a lasting effect on the growth of california. Do you think it was a positive effect

• question marks

THURSDAY   **WEEK 13**

Preview the 4 daily lessons to ensure you review or introduce skills that may be unfamiliar to students.

Electric Energy

You come home one evening in november. The house ~~are~~ is dark and cold mom unlocks the front door and you hurry inside. You fumble in the ~~darknes.~~ darkness until you find the switch. You flip the switch and the room fills with bright light. Mom walks over and flips another switch Hot air from an electric heater begins to ~~warme~~ warm the room. Have you ever wondered what life would be like without electricity?

Error Summary	
Capitalization	2
Language Usage	1
Punctuation:	
Comma	1
Period	3
Other	1
Spelling	2

MONDAY **WEEK 14**

Before people had electric energy at home they had to use candles or lanterns to light up the darkness. Houses ~~was~~ were heated by burning wood ~~inn~~ in stoves or fireplaces. fire was also used for cooking. Stoves were heated by burning wood, coal, or gas How do we cook today? Many stoves use heat from electric energy high-speed microwave ovens also use electric energy.

Error Summary	
Capitalization	2
Language Usage	1
Punctuation:	
Comma	3
Period	2
Other	1
Spelling	1

TUESDAY **WEEK 14**

Electric Energy

You come home one evening in november. The house are dark and cold mom unlocks the front door and you hurry inside. You fumble in the darknes. until you find the switch. You flip the switch and the room fills with bright light. Mom walks over and flips another switch Hot air from an electric heater begins to warme the room. Have you ever wondered what life would be like without electricity.

• question marks

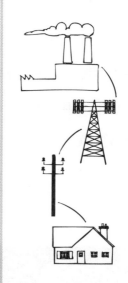

MONDAY **WEEK 14**

Before people had electric energy at home they had to use candles or lanterns to light up the darkness. Houses was heated by burning wood inn stoves or fireplaces. fire was also used for cooking. Stoves were heated by burning wood coal or gas How do we cook today. Many stoves use heat from electric energy high-speed microwave ovens also use electric energy.

• question marks

TUESDAY **WEEK 14**

Where does electric energie come from? How does power get to the electric outlets at your house? it all starts at a power plant. The power plant use energy to make electricity Some power plants use energy from flowing water to make electricity and some use energy from steam. This energy is used to make a machine spin? The spinning mashine uses wires and magnets to create a electric current.

Error Summary

Capitalization	1
Language Usage	2
Punctuation:	
Comma	1
Period	2
Other	2
Spelling	2

WEDNESDAY   **WEEK 14**

The electric curent made at the power plant flows through large wires these are called transmission lines The transmission lines carry the electric current to a energy substation? From there, the electric current flows through distribution lines. Have you see these lines? they is held up by poles. These lines carry electricity to your house that is how you get power when you flip a light switch.

Error Summary

Capitalization	3
Language Usage	3
Punctuation:	
Period	4
Other	1
Spelling	1

THURSDAY   **WEEK 14**

Name _____

Where does electric energie come from. How does power get to the electric outlets at your house it all starts at a power plant. The power plant use energy to make electricity Some power plants use energy from flowing water to make electricity and some use energy from steam. This energy is used to make a machine spin? The spinning mashine uses wires and magnets to create a electric current.

- question marks

WEDNESDAY　　　　　**WEEK 14**

The electric curent made at the power plant flows through large wires these are called transmission lines The transmission lines carry the electric current to a energy substation? From there, the electric current flows through distribution lines. Have you see these lines they is held up by poles. These lines carry electricity to your house that is how you get power when you flip a light switch.

- question marks

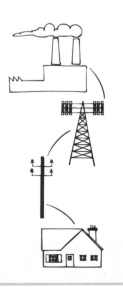

THURSDAY　　　　　**WEEK 14**

Preview the 4 daily lessons to ensure you review or introduce skills that may be unfamiliar to students.

A Woman of Science

Marie curie was born in warsaw poland, in 1867. As a young girl marie ~~like~~ liked science and she was an excellent student When Marie was older she wanted to study science and math at a college in warsaw. At that time however women ~~was~~ were not allowed to study at Polish colleges so marie continued to ~~studie~~ study and read textbooks on her own. She also studied with other ~~woman~~ women at a secret school.

Error Summary

Capitalization	6
Language Usage	3
Punctuation:	
Comma	7
Period	1
Spelling	1

MONDAY   **WEEK 15**

When marie curie was 24 she went to paris france to attend college she went to the Sorbonne a very well-known university. Curie didnt have as much science ~~traning~~ training as many of the other students. She had to work very hard but soon she was the best student in her class. curie graduated with a science degree in 1893. By the next year she had completed a second degree in math.

Error Summary

Capitalization	6
Punctuation:	
Apostrophe	1
Comma	6
Period	1
Spelling	1

TUESDAY   **WEEK 15**

Name _____

A Woman of Science

Marie curie was born in warsaw poland, in 1867. As a young girl marie like science and she was an excellent student When Marie was older she wanted to study science and math at a college in warsaw. At that time however women was not allowed to study at Polish colleges so marie continued to studie and read textbooks on her own. She also studied with other woman at a secret school.

• commas

MONDAY   **WEEK 15**

When marie curie was 24 she went to paris france to attend college she went to the Sorbonne a very well-known university. Curie didnt have as much science traning as many of the other students. She had to work very hard but soon she was the best student in her class. curie graduated with a science degree in 1893. By the next year she had completed a second degree in math.

• commas

TUESDAY   **WEEK 15**

　　　　　　　　　　　　　learned
　　　In 1896, curie ~~learn~~ of recent discoveries made

about the element uranium an element is a pure

substance that cannot be broken down any further.

　　　　　　scientist
Another ~~sientist~~ had discovered that uranium gave

　　　　　　　　　　　　　　　　　began
off a type of energy Marie curie ~~begun~~ studying

this energy She called it "radioactivity" she wanted to

find out how uranium was able to create radioactivity?

Error Summary

Capitalization	4
Language Usage	2
Punctuation:	
Period	5
Spelling	1

WEDNESDAY　　　　　　　　　　　　　　**WEEK 15**

　　　　　　　spent
　　　marie curie ~~spended~~ the rest of her life

studying radioactivity. She discovered that uranium

gives off radioactivity through its atoms curies work

helped scientists learn more about atoms? Even more

importantly, curie discovered two new elements and

they both were radioactive. By the end of her life

in 1934 marie curie had become the first woman to

receive a nobel Prize for her work.

Error Summary

Capitalization	7
Language Usage	1
Punctuation:	
Apostrophe	1
Comma	2
Period	2

THURSDAY　　　　　　　　　　　　　　**WEEK 15**

In 1896, curie learn of recent discoveries made about the element uranium an element is a pure substance that cannot be broken down any further. Another sientist had discovered that uranium gave off a type of energy Marie curie begun studying this energy She called it "radioactivity" she wanted to find out how uranium was able to create radioactivity?

• run-on sentences

WEDNESDAY   **WEEK 15**

marie curie spended the rest of her life studying radioactivity. She discovered that uranium gives off radioactivity through its atoms curies work helped scientists learn more about atoms? Even more importantly, curie discovered two new elements and they both were radioactive. By the end of her life in 1934 marie curie had become the first woman to receive a nobel Prize for her work.

• commas

THURSDAY   **WEEK 15**

Preview the 4 daily lessons to ensure you review or introduce skills that may be unfamiliar to students.

Terrific Teeth

Can you imagine having special tools to cut up all the foods that you eat? you'd need something sharp to cut off a slice of hard, crisp carrot. something pointy would help you pierce a firm, crunchy apple. You'd probably need something else, to help you work your way through a ~~delisious~~ delicious juicy piece of ~~stake~~ steak. Actually, you probably have a complete set of tools to do these jobs. The ~~tules~~ tools are your teeth!

Error Summary

Capitalization	2
Punctuation:	
Apostrophe	1
Comma	3
Period	1
Other	2
Spelling	3

MONDAY   **WEEK 16**

Grown-ups usually have a full set of 32 adult teeth. A full set for children is only 20 teeth, most children lose their primary teeth between ages 6 and 11. There are several ~~diffrent~~ different types of teeth. in the center of your mouth, you have 4 thin teeth on the top and 4 on the bottom. You use them to cut into hard, crunchy foods that you bite. These teeth are called incisors, babies often get these ~~teeth~~ teeth first.

Error Summary

Capitalization	3
Language Usage	1
Punctuation:	
Comma	2
Period	3
Spelling	1

TUESDAY   **WEEK 16**

EMC 2727 • Daily Paragraph Editing, Grade 4 • ©2004 by Evan-Moor Corp.

Name _____

Terrific Teeth

Can you imagine having special tools to cut up all the foods that you eat you'd need something sharp to cut off a slice of hard crisp carrot. something pointy would help you pierce a firm crunchy apple. Youd probably need something else. to help you work your way through a delisious juicy piece of stake. Actually, you probably have a complete set of tools to do these jobs. The tules are your teeth

• exclamation points

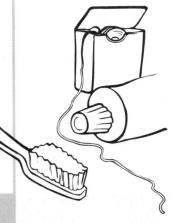

MONDAY   **WEEK 16**

Grown-ups usually have a full set of 32 adult teeth. A full set for children is only 20 teeth most children lose their primary teeth between ages 6 and 11. There are several diffrent types of teeth. in the center of your mouth you have 4 thin teeth on the top and 4 on the bottom. You use them to cut into hard crunchy foods that you bite. These teeth are called incisors babies often get these tooth first

• special words in quotes

TUESDAY   **WEEK 16**

There are 4 pointy teeth next to the incisors.
They ~~is~~ _are_ on the left and right sides of your mouth
there are 2 on top and 2 on the ~~botom~~ _bottom_. These sharp
pointy teeth are used for tearing food. They are
called canine teeth, or "eyeteeth." The rest of the
teeth are ~~widder~~ _wider_ and flatter. They are used to crush
and grind food these teeth are called molars. Molars
work hard to make it easier for us to digest our food.

Error Summary

Capitalization	2
Language Usage	1
Punctuation:	
Comma	1
Period	5
Quotation Mark	1
Spelling	2

WEDNESDAY   **WEEK 16**

~~Tooths~~ _Teeth_ do an important job in our bodies they
help us ~~brake~~ _break_ our food down into smaller pieces. this
makes it ~~easyer~~ _easier_ for the digestive system to do its
job. Its important to take care of our teeth. By
brushing and flossing after ~~meels~~ _meals_. If we dont brush,
food and germs left on our teeth can begin to cause
decay. Decay can weaken and destroy strong, healthy
teeth. So be sure to brush and floss, every day!

Error Summary

Capitalization	3
Language Usage	1
Punctuation:	
Apostrophe	2
Comma	2
Period	3
Other	1
Spelling	3

THURSDAY   **WEEK 16**

EMC 2727 • Daily Paragraph Editing, Grade 4 • ©2004 by Evan-Moor Corp.

Name _____

There are 4 pointy teeth next to the incisors. They is on the left and right sides of your mouth there are 2 on top and 2 on the botom These sharp pointy teeth are used for tearing food? They are called canine teeth, or eyeteeth." The rest of the teeth, are widder and flatter. They are used to crush and grind food these teeth are called molars. Molars work hard to make it easier for us to digest our food

WEDNESDAY   **WEEK 16**

Tooths do an important job in our bodies they help us brake our food down into smaller pieces. this makes it easyer for the digestive system to do its job. Its important to take care of our teeth. By brushing and flossing after meels. If we dont brush food and germs left on our teeth can begin to cause decay. Decay can weaken and destroy strong healthy teeth. So be sure to brush and floss. every day.

- exclamation points

THURSDAY   **WEEK 16**

Preview the 4 daily lessons to ensure you review or introduce skills that may be unfamiliar to students.

The Amazing Internet

Spring ~~brake~~ *break* is coming and ~~you're~~ *your* family is planning an outing to a local theme park. As you finalize your plans, there are some details to check. You want to find out about next weeks ~~wether~~ *weather* your parents need to get directions to the amusement park, and your brother wants to see how many roller coasters there are. Where can you go to find out everything in one place? just look on the Internet!

Error Summary

Capitalization	2
Punctuation:	
Apostrophe	1
Comma	2
Period	2
Other	1
Spelling	3

MONDAY   **WEEK 17**

a few years ago it would probably have ~~took~~ *taken* more time and effort to find all this information. You might have ~~find~~ *found* a long-range weather forecast in the newspaper. Your parents might have ~~studyed~~ *studied* a map to find the best route to the Park, and your brother would have telephoned the park. today, people can find this information on the internet from a computer at home, work, school, or the public library.

Error Summary

Capitalization	4
Language Usage	2
Punctuation:	
Comma	5
Spelling	1

TUESDAY   **WEEK 17**

The Amazing Internet

Spring brake is coming and you're family is planning an outing to a local theme park. As you finalize your plans there are some details to check You want to find out about next weeks wether your parents need to get directions to the amusement park and your brother wants to see how many roller coasters there are. Where can you go to find out everything in one place just look on the Internet!

MONDAY   **WEEK 17**

a few years ago it would probably have took more time and effort to find all this information. You might have find a long-range weather forecast in the newspaper. Your parents might have studied a map to find the best route to the Park and your brother would have telephoned the park. today, people can find this information on the internet from a computer at home work school or the public library.

TUESDAY   **WEEK 17**

The work that led to the creation of the
internet ~~begun~~ *began* in the 1960s. Most computers ~~was~~ *were*
used by the government**,** universities**,** and businesses.
The ~~u.s.~~ *U.S.* government was looking for a way to link
~~it's~~ *its* computers together so that information could be
easily shared. ~~b~~*B*y 1969, the first four computers had
been linked together in a network. Information flowed
between them**,** over telephone lines**.**

Error Summary
Capitalization	4
Language Usage	2
Punctuation:	
Apostrophe	1
Comma	2
Period	2

~~i~~*I*n the 1980s, people began to ~~bye~~ *buy* computers to
use at home**.** ~~m~~*M*ore computer networks were created**,**
and the early Internet ~~begun~~ *began* to grow. In order to
use the internet**,** users had to ~~tipe~~ *type* in complex codes.
Finally, in 1991, the World Wide Web was created~~?~~**.**
That made it ~~easyer~~ *easier* to use the internet. By 1995,
people could connect to the internet on their home
computers. A new era in information had ~~begin~~ *begun*.

Error Summary
Capitalization	5
Language Usage	2
Punctuation:	
Comma	2
Period	2
Spelling	3

Name _____

The work that led to the creation of the internet begun in the 1960s. Most computers was used by the government universities and businesses. The u.s. government was looking for a way to link it's computers together so that information could be easily shared. by 1969, the first four computers had been linked together in a network. Information flowed between them. over telephone lines

WEDNESDAY   **WEEK 17**

in the 1980s, people began to bye computers to use at home more computer networks were created and the early Internet begun to grow. In order to use the internet users had to tipe in complex codes. Finally, in 1991, the World Wide Web was created? That made it easyer to use the internet. By 1995, people could connect to the internet on their home computers. A new era in information had begin.

THURSDAY   **WEEK 17**

Preview the 4 daily lessons to ensure you review or introduce skills that may be unfamiliar to students.

Indiana Sundays

As a child, i adored summer sunday afternoons. At precisely twelve oclock the huge church bells rang out from the tower and the giant heavy doors swung open. Quick as a flash my cousins and i burst out into the bright hot afternoon. We'd pile into each others cars in a wild disorderly fashion. Grandma and grandpas farmhouse was our destination and eating lunch was our first mission. Yum!

Error Summary	
Capitalization	4
Punctuation:	
Apostrophe	3
Comma	7
Other	1

MONDAY   **WEEK 18**

Our noontime meal was large, loud and long. Once we were completely stuffed we slammed our way out grandmas back door. That is when the fun began. we chased barn cats stomped in cow pies and threw each other into haystacks. We explored every nook and cranny of grandpas weathered rickety barn we tossed one another into wheelbarrows and raced across the earthen hay-covered barn floor.

Error Summary	
Capitalization	4
Punctuation:	
Apostrophe	2
Comma	7
Period	1

TUESDAY   **WEEK 18**

Name —

Indiana Sundays

As a child, i adored summer sunday afternoons. At precisely twelve oclock the huge church bells rang out from the tower and the giant heavy doors swung open. Quick as a flash my cousins and i burst out into the bright hot afternoon. We'd pile into each others cars in a wild disorderly fashion. Grandma and grandpas farmhouse was our destination and eating lunch was our first mission. Yum

- commas

MONDAY   **WEEK 18**

Our noontime meal was large loud and long. Once we were completely stuffed we slammed our way out grandmas back door. That is when the fun began. we chased barn cats stomped in cow pies and threw each other into haystacks. We explored every nook and cranny of grandpas weathered rickety barn we tossed one another into wheelbarrows and raced across the earthen hay-covered barn floor.

- commas

TUESDAY   **WEEK 18**

Another favorite place to play was the basement⊙ no matter how many times we'd been down there‸ it always seemed like there was more to discover. Wow! There were flowers from grandmas garden‸ drying in the cramped quarters behind the enormous‸ massive furnace⊙ Shelves were lined with the vegetables that grandma began canning as soon as her garden yielded its usual bumper crop in late spring⊙

Error Summary

Capitalization	3
Punctuation:	
Apostrophe	1
Comma	2
Period	4
Other	1

WEDNESDAY   **WEEK 18**

As soon as night fell‸ we'd leave the dark‸ drafty basement for the yard. Catching fireflies was a favorite outdoor activity⊙ chasing each other through the yard playing nighttime tag was also popular. We knew it was time to go when grandpa began his nightly ritual of turning out the various lanterns around the farm. Under the pitch-black sky‸ we'd sadly say good-bye to one more indiana ~~sundae~~ Sunday.

Error Summary

Capitalization	4
Punctuation:	
Comma	3
Period	1
Spelling	1

THURSDAY   **WEEK 18**

Another favorite place to play was the basement no matter how many times we'd been down there it always seemed like there was more to discover. Wow There were flowers from grandmas garden. drying in the cramped quarters behind the enormous massive furnace Shelves were lined with the vegetables that grandma began canning as soon as her garden yielded its usual bumper crop in late spring

WATCH FOR

• commas

WEDNESDAY   **WEEK 18**

As soon as night fell we'd leave the dark drafty basement for the yard. Catching fireflies was a favorite outdoor activity chasing each other through the yard playing nighttime tag was also popular. We knew it was time to go when grandpa began his nightly ritual of turning out the various lanterns around the farm. Under the pitch-black sky we'd sadly say good-bye to one more indiana sundae.

WATCH FOR

• commas

THURSDAY   **WEEK 18**

Preview the 4 daily lessons to ensure you review or introduce skills that may be unfamiliar to students.

The View from Down Here

I was only three years old but i still remember
how I ~~feeled~~ (felt) on that day so long ago i can still see
how it all looked to me. My parents had ~~take~~ (taken) us
to the museum with them. They had been planning
this outing for days and it was a special occasion. I
remember that mom wore a blue dress and my Father
had on a ~~sute~~ (suit). My sister and ~~me~~ (I) wore matching
dresses and we had on our patent leather shoes

Error Summary	
Capitalization	4
Language Usage	3
Punctuation:	
Comma	4
Period	2
Spelling	1

MONDAY   **WEEK 19**

There must have been a special exhibit at the
museum it was very ~~crouded~~ (crowded) and my sister and ~~me~~ (I)
bumped into strangers as we trailed after our parents.
from one room to another. Was it ~~a~~ (an) exhibit of
paintings or of sculpture? i cannot remember what I
do remember is growing restless as I ~~taggd~~ (tagged) after my
parents in that crowded stuffy place. Ugh!

Error Summary	
Capitalization	3
Language Usage	2
Punctuation:	
Comma	2
Period	3
Other	2
Spelling	2

TUESDAY   **WEEK 19**

The View from Down Here

I was only three years old but i still remember how I feeled on that day so long ago i can still see how it all looked to me. My parents had take us to the museum with them. They had been planning this outing for days and it was a special occasion. I remember that mom wore a blue dress and my Father had on a sute. My sister and me wore matching dresses and we had on our patent leather shoes

• commas

MONDAY   **WEEK 19**

There must have been a special exhibit at the museum it was very crouded and my sister and me bumped into strangers as we trailed after our parents. from one room to another. Was it a exhibit of paintings or of sculpture i cannot remember what I do remember is growing restless as I taggd after my parents in that crowded stuffy place. Ugh

• question marks
• exclamation points

TUESDAY   **WEEK 19**

I'm not sure when I realized that i was alone. When I looked around, I could not see my Mother, father, or sister any where. Panic came over me as I wondered wonder which way they had gone. I felt relieved when I saw my father's familiar shoes with the pattern of swirling dots across the toe. I rushed over to stand next to those shoes shoose. I took hold of the large warm hand that hung down near my shoulder.

Error Summary

Capitalization	2
Language Usage	1
Punctuation:	
Apostrophe	2
Comma	3
Period	2
Spelling	2

WEDNESDAY   **WEEK 19**

My relief quickly turned to surprise serprise and then embarrassment as I looked up at the man standing in those familiar shoes. It was not my father at all. Oh, no! Who was this total stranger? I burst bursted into tears and started to run. Suddenly, i was swept up into my mother's arms in a comforting hug. When she heard herd the commotion, she came come to my rescue. the concerned stranger looked at me. Then he smiled. so did i.

Error Summary

Capitalization	6
Language Usage	2
Punctuation:	
Apostrophe	1
Comma	1
Period	2
Other	2
Spelling	2

THURSDAY   **WEEK 19**

Im not sure when I realized that i was alone.
When I looked around I could not see my Mother
father or sister any where. Panic came over me as I
wonder which way they had gone I felt relieved when
I saw my fathers familiar shoes with the pattern of
swirling dots. across the toe. I rushed over to stand
next to those shoose. I took hold of the large warm
hand that hung down near my shoulder.

- commas
- apostrophes

WEDNESDAY   **WEEK 19**

My relief quickly turned to serprise and then
embarrassment as I looked up. At the man standing
in those familiar shoes. It was not my Father at all.
Oh, no Who was this total stranger. I bursted into
tears and started to run. Suddenly, i was swept up
into my mothers arms in a comforting hug. When
she herd the commotion she come to my rescue. the
concerned stranger looked at me. Then he smiled.
so did i

- exclamation points
- spelling

THURSDAY   **WEEK 19**

Preview the 4 daily lessons to ensure you review or introduce skills that may be unfamiliar to students.

An American Classic

Little house on the prairie is the second book in the autobiographical series by beloved american author laura ingalls wilder. The first book, Little house in the big woods is the story of lauras childhood in the wisconsin woods. Laura was seven years old when her familee [family] moved from wisconsin to kansas. she traviled [traveled] in a covered wagon with ma pa older sister mary and baby carrie.

Error Summary	
Capitalization	18
Punctuation:	
Apostrophe	1
Comma	5
Other	1
Spelling	2

MONDAY　　　　　　　　　　　**WEEK 20**

The early part of the book describes everyday life during the families [family's] trip. We see how pa took a brake [break] from driving the wagon to stop and hunt for food. Ma cooked the meals and she even did the familys laundry Laura and mary enjoyed all the new sights and sounds of the prairie and Ma had fun watching them chase prairie hens and their chicks.

Error Summary	
Capitalization	2
Punctuation:	
Apostrophe	1
Comma	2
Period	1
Spelling	2

TUESDAY　　　　　　　　　　　**WEEK 20**

Name _____

An American Classic

<u>Little house on the prairie</u> is the second book in the autobiographical series by beloved american author laura ingalls wilder. The first book Little house in the big woods is the story of lauras childhood in the wisconsin woods. Laura was seven years old when her familee moved from wisconsin to kansas. she traviled in a covered wagon with ma pa older sister mary and baby carrie.

• book titles
• commas

| MONDAY | WEEK 20 |

The early part of the book describes everyday life during the families trip. We see how pa took a brake from driving the wagon to stop and hunt for food. Ma cooked the meals and she even did the familys laundry Laura and mary enjoyed all the new sights and sounds of the prairie and Ma had fun watching them chase prairie hens and their chicks.

• apostrophes

| TUESDAY | WEEK 20 |

The family finally reached a place on the prairie where they decided to settle the next part of the book describes all the stages of building a log house and its furnishings, and it also describes ~~bilding~~ building a stable. Laura described the family's daily life, and she explained the chores done by each member of the family. Readers will see the difference, between modern-day and pioneer life.

Error Summary

Capitalization	1
Punctuation:	
Apostrophe	1
Comma	2
Period	3
Spelling	1

WEDNESDAY   **WEEK 20**

By the end of Little house on the prairie, the american government had decided that settlers could not remain in the area of kansas known as Indian territory. Once again, the ingalls family packed up their covered wagon, and moved on. Readers can join the family as they move to a new home and new adventures in minnesota. just read On the Banks of Plum Creek, the next book in the series.

Error Summary

Capitalization	9
Punctuation:	
Comma	2
Period	2
Other	2

THURSDAY   **WEEK 20**

The family finally reached a place on the prairie where they decided to settle the next part of the book describes all the stages of building a log house and its furnishings and it also describes bilding a stable. Laura described the familys daily life and she explained the chores done by each member of the family? Readers will see the difference. between modern-day and pioneer life.

WATCH FOR

• commas

WEDNESDAY   **WEEK 20**

By the end of Little house on the prairie the american government had decided that settlers could not remain in the area of kansas known as Indian territory. Once again, the ingalls family packed up their covered wagon. And moved on. Readers can join the family as they move to a new home and new adventures in minnesota just read On the Banks of Plum Creek the next book in the series.

WATCH FOR

• book titles
• special words in quotes

THURSDAY   **WEEK 20**

Preview the 4 daily lessons to ensure you review or introduce skills that may be unfamiliar to students.

Bored in Space

passed

Four years had ~~past~~ since we blasted off Worim. All the planets in our star system were so crowded that we couldnt find a place to land we wanted to stay on Worim but it was too dangerous.

"the worms have eaten everything that was green and most things that arent," mom said. "we could be next"

We've got to find a new planet where we can settle said dad.

Error Summary	
Capitalization	5
Punctuation:	
Apostrophe	3
Comma	2
Period	2
Quotation Mark	2
Spelling	1

MONDAY   **WEEK 21**

onboard

I had read all the books that we had ~~onbored~~ our craft and our communication system didnt offer much entertainment. There was so much litter cluttering deep space that we could barely pick up the important space traffic messages? i was getting pretty tired of the same old dull boring routine every day!

There must be something you can do in the science lab Robin, mom finally suggested one day

Error Summary	
Capitalization	2
Punctuation:	
Apostrophe	1
Comma	3
Period	2
Quotation Mark	2
Spelling	1

TUESDAY   **WEEK 21**

                      EMC 2727 • Daily Paragraph Editing, Grade 4 • ©2004 by Evan-Moor Corp.

Name _____

Bored in Space

Four years had past since we blasted off Worim. All the planets in our star system were so crowded that we couldnt find a place to land we wanted to stay on Worim but it was too dangerous.

"the worms have eaten everything that was green and most things that arent," mom said. "we could be next"

Weve got to find a new planet where we can settle. said dad.

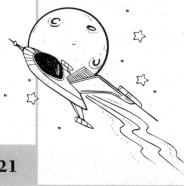

MONDAY   **WEEK 21**

I had read all the books that we had onbored our craft and our communication system didnt offer much entertainment. There was so much litter cluttering deep space that we could barely pick up the important space traffic messages? i was getting pretty tired of the same old dull boring routine every day!

There must be something you can do in the science lab Robin, mom finally suggested one day

TUESDAY   **WEEK 21**

"Well, mom, what did you have in mind?" I asked as we entered the lab together.

"Robin, remember good old Grow-Bot?" Mom asked. She pointed toward a metal form. It was partly covered by a ~~peace~~ piece of cloth.

"Mom, do you think i could forget my computer tutor?" I replied as i uncovered the machine that i practically ~~new~~ knew by heart.

Error Summary

Capitalization	6
Punctuation:	
Comma	4
Period	3
Quotation Mark	2
Other	2
Spelling	2

WEDNESDAY   **WEEK 21**

"You know, Robin, you've learned so much about computers lately," Mom remarked. "Remember how you helped dad reprogram the autopilot function last month?"

"Mom, do you ~~reely~~ really think I could reprogram Grow-Bot?" I asked.

"You might as well try, robin," mom said cheerfully.

"You know, mom," I said, "I think this could turn out to be fun."

Error Summary

Capitalization	5
Punctuation:	
Comma	7
Period	3
Quotation Mark	5
Other	1
Spelling	1

THURSDAY   **WEEK 21**

• dialog
• spelling

"Well mom what did you have in mind" I asked as we entered the lab together

Robin remember good old Grow-Bot? Mom asked. She pointed toward a metal form it was partly covered by a peace of cloth.

"mom do you think i could forget my computer tutor" I replied as i uncovered the machine that i practically new by heart

WEDNESDAY   **WEEK 21**

• dialog

"You know Robin you've learned so much about computers lately, Mom remarked remember how you helped dad reprogram the autopilot function last month"

"Mom do you reely think I could reprogram Grow-Bot? I asked

You might as well try robin" mom said cheerfully.

"You know mom" I said, I think this could turn out to be fun"

THURSDAY   **WEEK 21**

Preview the 4 daily lessons to ensure you review or introduce skills that may be unfamiliar to students.

Schools Should Lead by Example

believe

i beleave schools should lead the way in caring for our environment for example, many children eat a school lunch. Every day and school kitchens all over our nation make these lunches. Unfortunately, most school lunches are packaged in materials made from nonrenewable resources. Plastic packages, aluminum foil and plastic silverware all use nonrenewable resources.

creates

This also create waste in our landfills.

Error Summary	
Capitalization	3
Language Usage	1
Punctuation:	
Comma	3
Period	4
Spelling	1

MONDAY   **WEEK 22**

products

Schools should use product made from recycled and renewable materials there are many new types of food packages made of recyclable materials. For instance, if schools used cardboard packaging for lunches they could recycle thousands of packages every day Also, think of all the paper that schools

recycled

use if every school across the nation recycle paper countless trees could be saved.

Error Summary	
Capitalization	2
Language Usage	2
Punctuation:	
Comma	2
Period	5

TUESDAY   **WEEK 22**

Schools Should Lead by Example

• commas

i beleave schools should lead the way in caring for our environment for example, many children eat a school lunch. Every day and school kitchens all over our nation make these lunches. Unfortunately, most school lunches are packaged in materials made from nonrenewable resources Plastic packages aluminum foil and plastic silverware all use nonrenewable resources. This also create waste in our landfills

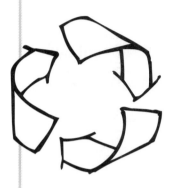

MONDAY   **WEEK 22**

• run-on sentences
• commas

Schools should use product made from recycled and renewable materials there are many new types of food packages made of recyclable materials For instance, if schools used cardboard packaging for lunches they could recycle thousands of packages every day Also, think of all the paper that schools use if every school across the nation recycle paper countless trees could be saved

TUESDAY   **WEEK 22**

schools should make sure that every classroom has several recycle bins so paper, plastic, aluminum, and glass can all be recycled. many student (students) already recycle at home. Dont schools think that he (they) should set a good example and practice recycling, too? Another way that schools can set a good example is to have an environmental awareness program. They can plan a whole week of activities for students.

Error Summary

Capitalization	2
Language Usage	3
Punctuation:	
Apostrophe	1
Comma	3
Period	1
Other	1

WEDNESDAY   **WEEK 22**

on monday, students could plant trees. Since it takes 17 trees to make one ton of paper, planting would help replace this renewable resource. On tuesday, schools could challenge students to a "zero garbage" day. the goal would be to see if students can use recyclable and reusable materials to avoid creating waiste (waste) products. schools should leed (lead) by example and motivate students to care for our planet.

Error Summary

Capitalization	5
Punctuation:	
Comma	1
Period	3
Spelling	2

THURSDAY   **WEEK 22**

Name _____

schools should make sure that every classroom has several recycle bins so paper plastic aluminum and glass can all be recycled. many student already recycle at home. Dont schools think that he should set a good example and practice recycling, too. Another way that schools can set a good example is to have a environmental awareness program. They can plan a whole week of activities for students

- commas

WEDNESDAY   **WEEK 22**

---

on monday, students could plant trees Since it takes 17 trees to make one ton of paper planting would help replace this renewable resource. On tuesday, schools could challenge students to a "zero garbage" day the goal would be to see if students can use recyclable and reusable materials to avoid creating waiste products. schools should leed by example and motivate students to care for our planet

- run-on sentences

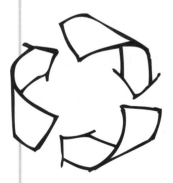

THURSDAY   **WEEK 22**

Preview the 4 daily lessons to ensure you review or introduce skills that may be unfamiliar to students.

Blackbeard the Pirate

nobody knows just when edward teach became
known
~~know~~ as Blackbeard the Pirate we do know though
that edward teach joined Captain benjamin Hornigold's
                                        whether
crew in 1716. It is unclear ~~weather~~ teach knew that
capt hornigold planned to raid ships in the caribbean
Sea. However, teach helped hornigold capture a french
ship in the Caribbean in 1717

Error Summary

Capitalization	14
Language Usage	1
Punctuation:	
Comma	2
Period	3
Spelling	1

MONDAY   **WEEK 23**

Capt hornigold gave the captured french ship to
                            changed
edward Teach. The ships name was ~~change~~ to Queen
anne's Revenge and she soon was feared as a dreaded
pirate ship. Edward teach also changed his name The
pirate Captain of Queen Annes Revenge was now called
"blackbeard." When he took his fierce colorful name
Blackbeard also changed the way he looked

Error Summary

Capitalization	7
Language Usage	1
Punctuation:	
Apostrophe	2
Comma	3
Period	3
Other	1

TUESDAY   **WEEK 23**

Blackbeard the Pirate

nobody knows just when edward teach became know as Blackbeard the Pirate we do know though that edward teach joined Captain benjamin Hornigold's crew in 1716. It is unclear weather teach knew that capt hornigold planned to raid ships in the caribbean Sea. However, teach helped hornigold capture a french ship in the Caribbean in 1717

- names of people
- names of places

MONDAY   **WEEK 23**

Capt hornigold gave the captured french ship to edward Teach. The ships name was change to <u>Queen anne's Revenge</u> and she soon was feared as a dreaded pirate ship. Edward teach also changed his name The pirate Captain of Queen Annes Revenge was now called "blackbeard." When he took his fierce colorful name Blackbeard also changed the way he looked

- names of people
- names of ships

TUESDAY   **WEEK 23**

Blackbeard let his beard grow out to a frizzy bushy tangle he wove braids into his beard and he even ~~tyed~~ tied them with ribbons. He stuck fuses from cannons under his pirate hat. These fuses were made of string soaked in ~~watter~~ water mixed with gunpowder When blackbeard lit the fuses they sizzled and ~~smoaked~~ smoked and their ghostly light and foul gassy smell scared his victims

Error Summary

Capitalization	2
Punctuation:	
Comma	5
Period	3
Spelling	3

WEDNESDAY   **WEEK 23**

In the summer of 1718 blackbeard sank queen Annes' revenge off the coast of North carolina. However, he still had other ships to use in ~~rades~~ raids along the coast. people decided that this terror must stop so Lieutenant robert Maynard organized a secret mission to capture blackbeard. The fierce bearded pirate battled to the ~~deth~~ death and was beheaded by the victorious Lt. maynard.

Error Summary

Capitalization	8
Punctuation:	
Apostrophe	1
Comma	3
Other	1
Spelling	2

THURSDAY   **WEEK 23**

EMC 2727 • Daily Paragraph Editing, Grade 4 • ©2004 by Evan-Moor Corp.

Blackbeard let his beard grow out to a frizzy bushy tangle he wove braids into his beard and he even tyed them with ribbons. He stuck fuses from cannons under his pirate hat. These fuses were made of string soaked in watter mixed with gunpowder When blackbeard lit the fuses they sizzled and smoaked and their ghostly light and foul gassy smell scared his victims

- commas

WEDNESDAY **WEEK 23**

In the summer of 1718 blackbeard sank queen Annes' revenge off the coast of North carolina. However, he still had other ships to use in rades along the coast. people decided that this terror must stop so Lieutenant robert Maynard organized a secret mission to capture blackbeard. The fierce bearded pirate battled to the deth and was beheaded by the victorious Lt. maynard.

- names of people
- names of ships

THURSDAY **WEEK 23**

Preview the 4 daily lessons to ensure you review or introduce skills that may be unfamiliar to students.

A Gifted Girl

Ballerina maria tallchief was born on a indian reservation in oklahoma in 1925. Her Fathers family was from the Osage tribe her Mothers' ancestors were from scotland and ireland. The osage once hunt buffalo and gathered food in the area that is now arkansas, kansas missouri and oklahoma. After taking most of their land the U.S. goverment moved the osage to a reservation in oklahoma

Error Summary	
Capitalization	16
Language Usage	2
Punctuation:	
Apostrophe	2
Comma	3
Period	2
Spelling	1

MONDAY   **WEEK 24**

After oil was found on the osage reservation in the late 1800s the tribe became very welthy. Marias father Alex tallchief always had a very comfortable life because of this. He feeled he did not need to go to college or have an career. marias mother Ruth tallchief wanted her children to learn as much as possible. So maria and marjorie her younger sister began music and dance lessons at around age three

Error Summary	
Capitalization	6
Language Usage	2
Punctuation:	
Apostrophe	2
Comma	7
Period	1
Spelling	1

TUESDAY   **WEEK 24**

Name _____

A Gifted Girl

Ballerina maria tallchief was born on a indian reservation in oklahoma in 1925. Her Fathers family was from the Osage tribe her Mothers' ancestors were from scotland and ireland. The osage once hunt buffalo and gathered food in the area that is now arkansas, kansas missouri and oklahoma. After taking most of their land the U.S. goverment moved the osage to a reservation in oklahoma

WATCH FOR

- commas
- names of people
- names of places

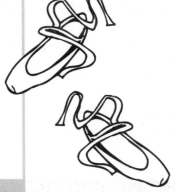

MONDAY	**WEEK 24**

After oil was found on the osage reservation in the late 1800s the tribe became very welthy. Marias father Alex tallchief always had a very comfortable life because of this. He feeled he did not need to go to college or have an career. marias mother Ruth tallchief wanted her children to learn as much as possible. So maria and marjorie her younger sister began music and dance lessons at around age three

WATCH FOR

- commas
- names of people
- names of places

TUESDAY	**WEEK 24**

even when they ~~was~~ [were] quite young. Both maria and her sister showed great promise in music and dance. Their mother ~~desided~~ [decided] the family should move to los angeles california. She ~~beleived~~ [believed] that her daughters would have a better chance to develop their talents in hollywood. The family made the move when maria was entering second grade.

Error Summary	
Capitalization	9
Language Usage	1
Punctuation:	
Comma	2
Period	1
Spelling	2

WEDNESDAY   **WEEK 24**

Maria began to focus on dance more than music. she started studying with a famous russian ballerina, Bronislava Nijinska. She ~~studyed~~ [studied] with madame nijinska for five years until finishing high school. She was then invited to ~~preform~~ [perform] with a professional ballet company. This was the start of her brilliant, successful career as a "prima ballerina," or ballet star.

Error Summary	
Capitalization	4
Punctuation:	
Comma	2
Period	1
Spelling	2

THURSDAY   **WEEK 24**

even when they was quite young Both maria and her sister showed great promise in music and dance. Their mother desided the family should move to los angeles california. She beleived that her daughters would have a better chance to develop their talents In hollywood. The family made the move when maria was entering second grade

• commas

WEDNESDAY   **WEEK 24**

Maria began to focus on dance more than music she started studying with a famous russian ballerina Bronislava Nijinska. She studyed with madame nijinska for five years until finishing high school. She was then invited to preform with a professional ballet company. This was the start of her brilliant successful career as a "prima ballerina," or ballet star.

• commas

THURSDAY   **WEEK 24**

Preview the 4 daily lessons to ensure you review or introduce skills that may be unfamiliar to students.

C. J. Clark Has Another Hit

it looks like author C. j. clark has another big hit! Her latest book ~~are~~ is Sarah Roth and the Wisdom Crystal. This is the third book in the series published by Creative book press. Sarah Roth and the Wisdom Crystal has the same ten-year-old heroine from clark's first ~~to~~ two books. If you enjoyed Clark's other adventure tales, you'll love Sarah Roth and the wisdom crystal.

Error Summary

Capitalization	8
Language Usage	1
Punctuation:	
Apostrophe	1
Comma	1
Period	2
Other	2
Spelling	1

MONDAY   **WEEK 25**

Like the other books in the series, sarah roth and the wisdom crystal is a magical adventure. Once again, the author ~~mix~~ mixes modern science with fantasy. she also introduces some unusual, exciting characters. Sarah's Aunt, Professor Eudora Vista, is a scientist. she studies rocks in the New mexico desert. The tale actually takes place during Sarah's summer vacation in New Mexico.

Error Summary

Capitalization	8
Language Usage	1
Punctuation:	
Apostrophe	1
Comma	3
Period	3

TUESDAY   **WEEK 25**

Name _____

C. J. Clark Has Another Hit

it looks like author C j clark has another big hit! Her latest book are <u>Sarah Roth and the Wisdom Crystal</u>. This is the third book in the series published by Creative book press. Sarah Roth and the Wisdom Crystal has the same ten-year-old heroine from clark's first to books. If you enjoyed Clarks other adventure tales you'll love Sarah Roth and the wisdom crystal.

WATCH FOR

• book titles
• abbreviations

MONDAY   **WEEK 25**

Like the other books in the series <u>sarah roth and the wisdom crystal</u> is a magical adventure. Once again, the author mix modern science with fantasy she also introduces some unusual exciting characters. Sarah's Aunt, Professor Eudora Vista is a scientist she studies rocks in the New mexico desert. The tale actually takes place during Sarahs summer vacation in New Mexico

WATCH FOR

• book titles
• commas

TUESDAY   **WEEK 25**

Another interesting colorful character is eleven-year-old Red Bird Roybal. The "wisdom crystal" in the books title belongs to him his grandfather a wise Pueblo elder gave it to him. sarah and her Aunt meet red bird on one of their rock-gathering trips. When prof Vista tries to learn more about Red Birds rare crystal they travel to another dimension where an amazing adventure begins

Error Summary

Capitalization	6
Punctuation:	
Apostrophe	2
Comma	4
Period	3

WEDNESDAY   **WEEK 25**

Lets hope nobody tries to make <u>Sarah Roth And The Wisdom Crystal</u> into a movie. Chances are it would be just as ~~week~~ weak as the movie version of <u>Sarah Roth and the Star Seeker</u>. That book did not work well in the film version? Readers will be better off just imagining the scenes in book three all of cj clarks books offer great food for childrens active eager imaginations.

Error Summary

Capitalization	6
Punctuation:	
Apostrophe	3
Comma	1
Period	4
Other	2
Spelling	1

THURSDAY   **WEEK 25**

Another interesting colorful character is eleven-year-old Red Bird Roybal. The "wisdom crystal" in the books title belongs to him his grandfather a wise Pueblo elder gave it to him. sarah and her Aunt meet red bird on one of their rock-gathering trips. When prof Vista tries to learn more about Red Birds rare crystal they travel to another dimension where an amazing adventure begins

• commas

WEDNESDAY   **WEEK 25**

Lets hope nobody tries to make Sarah Roth And The Wisdom Crystal into a movie. Chances are it would be just as week as the movie version of Sarah Roth and the Star Seeker. That book did not work well in the film version? Readers will be better off just imagining the scenes in book three all of c j clarks books offer great food for childrens active eager imaginations.

• book titles
• apostrophes

THURSDAY   **WEEK 25**

Preview the 4 daily lessons to ensure you review or introduce skills that may be unfamiliar to students.

Atlantic Oil Spill Threatens Spanish Coast

La Coruña, spain   november 19 2002

The Prestige, a damaged oil tanker that was leaking fuel oil off the coast of spain split in two and sank this morning. The tanker ran into trouble last week During stormy seas off northwestern spain the Prestige was carrying 77,000 tons of heavy fuel oil about 5,000 tons have already leaked out in an area known as the Coast of Death.

Error Summary

Capitalization	7
Language Usage	1
Punctuation:	
Comma	2
Period	3
Other	1
Spelling	2

MONDAY   **WEEK 26**

The spanish government took immediate action to protect the coastal area Floating barriers were set up in an effort to save the rich fishing grounds And delicate marine ecosystems that are at risk. The world community has been quick to respond to Spains call for help clean-up experts from the Netherlands are working on the disaster special tugboats were needed to tow the ship away from the shoreline

Error Summary

Capitalization	4
Language Usage	2
Punctuation:	
Apostrophe	1
Period	5
Spelling	1

TUESDAY   **WEEK 26**

Name _____

Atlantic Oil Spill Threatens Spanish Coast

• names of ships

La Coruña, spain   november 19 2002

The <u>Prestige</u>, a damaged oil tanker that was leeking fuel oil off the coast of spain split in two and sank this morning. The tanker ran into trouble last weak. During stormy seas off northwestern spain the Prestige was carrying 77,000 tons of heavy fuel oil about 5,000 tons have already leaked out in a area known as the Coast of Death.

MONDAY   **WEEK 26**

The spanish government took immediate action to protect the coastal area Floating barriers were set up in a effort to save the rich fishing grounds. And delicate marine ecosystems that are at risk. The world community has been quick to respond to Spains call for help clean-up experts from the Netherlands is working on the disaster? special tugboats were needed to toe the ship away from the shoreline

TUESDAY   **WEEK 26**

the <u>prestige</u> had been towed about 70 miles out to ~~see~~ sea before it shuddered, split in two, and sank today in atlantic waters that are over 2 miles deep. The ship still has some 72,000 tons of fuel oil In its tanks. If the fuel leaks, it could create the largest oil spill ever. The World Wildlife Fund, an ~~a~~ environmental group, warned that oil from the Prestige would create a spill twice as large as Alaskas' 1989 disaster.

Error Summary	
Capitalization	4
Language Usage	1
Punctuation:	
Apostrophe	1
Comma	5
Period	2
Other	2
Spelling	1

WEDNESDAY   **WEEK 26**

Expert's hope that the cold waters of the atlantic will cause the heavy fuel oil to ~~thikken~~ thicken. oil has never before been removed from tanks that have ~~sink~~ sunk so deep in the sea. Special gear and salvage methods may have to be ~~create~~ created to remove the fuel from the tanks. as experts search for solutions, they fear that the many rare coral and fish species in this habitat ~~mite~~ might never recover from the effects of a spill.

Error Summary	
Capitalization	3
Language Usage	2
Punctuation:	
Comma	1
Period	3
Spelling	3

THURSDAY   **WEEK 26**

Name _____

the prestige had been towed about 70 miles out to see before it shuddered split in two and sank today in atlantic waters that are over 2 miles deep. The ship still has some 72,000 tons of fuel oil. In its tanks. If the fuel leaks it could create the largest oil spill ever. The World Wildlife Fund a environmental group warned that oil from the Prestige would create a spill twice as large as Alaskas' 1989 disaster

WATCH FOR
- names of ships
- commas

WEDNESDAY   **WEEK 26**

Expert's hope that the cold waters of the atlantic will cause the heavy fuel oil to thikken oil has never before been removed from tanks that have sink so deep in the sea. Special gear and salvage methods may have to be create to remove the fuel from the tanks? as experts search for solutions they fear that the many rare coral and fish species in this habitat mite never recover from the effects of a spill

THURSDAY   **WEEK 26**

Preview the 4 daily lessons to ensure you review or introduce skills that may be unfamiliar to students.

Earth on the Move

People have been making ~~discoverys~~ discoveries about Earth for as long as ~~human~~ humans have lived ~~hear~~ here. ~~s~~ometimes, ~~P~~eople have to let go of their old-fashioned, widely accepted beliefs before they can ~~except~~ accept new ideas⊙ ~~f~~or example, many people in the late 1400s believed that Earth was flat⊙ Some people were not convinced that Earth was round⊙ until ships made it safely all the way around the world.

Error Summary

Capitalization	3
Language Usage	1
Punctuation:	
Comma	1
Period	3
Spelling	3

MONDAY   **WEEK 27**

For many years, people who ~~studyed~~ studied maps of the world saw something interesting. ~~t~~hey ~~notice~~ noticed that the shapes of some of the continents seemed to match. It looked like they were shaped to fit together, ~~J~~ust like puzzle ~~peices~~ pieces. In the early 1800s, an explorer found rocks in ~~s~~outh ~~a~~merica that looked like rocks in ~~a~~frica. ~~s~~cientists have ~~find~~ found several other similarities between the two continents⊙

Error Summary

Capitalization	6
Language Usage	2
Punctuation:	
Comma	1
Period	1
Spelling	2

TUESDAY   **WEEK 27**

Earth on the Move

• spelling

People have been making discoverys about Earth for as long as human have lived hear. sometimes, People have to let go of their old-fashioned widely accepted beliefs before they can except new ideas for example, many people in the late 1400s believed that Earth was flat Some people were not convinced that Earth was round. until ships made it safely all the way around the world.

MONDAY   **WEEK 27**

• verb tense

For many years, people who studyed maps of the world saw something interesting. they notice that the shapes of some of the continents seemed to match. It looked like they were shaped to fit together, Just like puzzle peices. In the early 1800s an explorer found rocks in south america that looked like rocks in africa. scientists have find several other similarities between the two continents

TUESDAY   **WEEK 27**

In the early 1900s a man named alfred wegener noticed something interesting. wegener studied [studied] the mountain ranges of south america and Africa he fit the two continents together as if they were puzzle pieces. He saw that the mountain ranges lined up wegener believe [believed] that these continents had once been one continuous solid mass of land that had broke [broken] apart

WEDNESDAY   **WEEK 27**

When wegener died in 1930 scientists did not yet accept his ideas. They did not believe that Earths continents had ever been joined in unfamiliar differently shaped masses in the 1960s, scientists had new information that proved wegeners' ideas were correct. They learned that Earth is made up of huge masses of rock called "plates." when the plates move the continents on top of the plates move, too

THURSDAY   **WEEK 27**

In the early 1900s a man named alfred wegener noticed something interesting. wegener studied the mountain ranges of south america and Africa he fit the two continents together as if they were puzzle pieces. He saw that the mountain ranges lined up wegener believe that these continents had once been one continuous solid mass of land that had broke apart

- commas

WEDNESDAY   **WEEK 27**

When wegener died in 1930 scientists did not yet accept his ideas. They did not believe that Earths continents had ever been joined in unfamiliar differently shaped masses in the 1960s, scientists had new information that proved wegeners' ideas were correct. They learned that Earth is made up of huge masses of rock called plates." when the plates move the continents on top of the plates move, too

- commas
- apostrophes

THURSDAY   **WEEK 27**

Preview the 4 daily lessons to ensure you review or introduce skills that may be unfamiliar to students.

A Journey Begins

I didn't want to let go but mr. O'Brien gently moved me away from Mother. "There now bridget, he said. I'll be leaving you behind if you don't hurry." He picked me up and set me in the wagon next to paul my brother.

Mother took off her shawl and wrapped me in it. "a little bit of ireland to have with you on the ship Bridget, she said thru her tears.

through

Error Summary

Capitalization	5
Punctuation:	
Comma	4
Quotation Mark	3
Spelling	1

MONDAY   **WEEK 28**

Take good care of them, mary finney, mother called out.

"Like my own, molly don't you worry," mary replied. I'll take them to your brother as soon as we reach boston"

Our bags of rough scratchy burlap were filled with food for the long journie. it was all mother could spare. The potatoe crop had rotted so all the wheat we raised went to pay the tax collector.

journey

potato

Error Summary

Capitalization	9
Punctuation:	
Comma	3
Period	3
Quotation Mark	3
Spelling	2

TUESDAY   **WEEK 28**

Name _____

A Journey Begins

I didn't want to let go but mr. O'Brien gently moved me away from Mother. "There now bridget, he said. I'll be leaving you behind if you don't hurry." He picked me up and set me in the wagon next to paul my brother.

Mother took off her shawl and wrapped me in it. "a little bit of ireland to have with you on the ship Bridget, she said thru her tears.

• dialog

MONDAY   **WEEK 28**

Take good care of them mary finney, mother called out.

"Like my own, molly don't you worry," mary replied. I'll take them to your brother as soon as we reach boston"

Our bags of rough scratchy burlap were filled with food for the long journie. it was all mother could spare. The potatoe crop had rotted so all the wheat we raised went to pay the tax collector

• dialog

TUESDAY   **WEEK 28**

Uncle james, mothers brother sailed to america two years ago. He sent mother some money for us to join him but there wasn't enough for all of us to go to america. When mary mothers friend was leaving to join her husband in boston, mother decided it would be better for us there. She promised she would come later meanwhile, uncle James would care for us.

Error Summary	
Capitalization	11
Punctuation:	
Apostrophe	2
Comma	4
Period	1

WEDNESDAY   **WEEK 28**

It was a tiring bumpy journey to the ship that would take us to america. As the wagon bounced along the road I turned to look at my brother. Paul, who was only eight years old, had started to cry. I reached out my hand and clasped his and he moved even closer to me. "We're together," I said softly in his ear. We'll help each other. We'll be just fine." Deep in my heart i knew then that we would be.

Error Summary	
Capitalization	2
Punctuation:	
Comma	4
Quotation Mark	1

THURSDAY   **WEEK 28**

Name _____

Uncle james, mothers brother sailed to america two years ago. He sent mother some money for us to join him but there wasn't enough for all of us to go to america. When mary mothers friend was leaving to join her husband in boston, mother decided it would be better for us there. She promised she would come later meanwhile, uncle James would care for us.

WATCH FOR

• commas
• names of people

WEDNESDAY   **WEEK 28**

It was a tiring bumpy journey to the ship that would take us to america. As the wagon bounced along the road I turned to look at my brother. Paul, who was only eight years old, had started to cry. I reached out my hand and clasped his and he moved even closer to me. "We're together," I said softly in his ear. We'll help each other. We'll be just fine." Deep in my heart i knew then that we would be.

WATCH FOR

• commas

THURSDAY   **WEEK 28**

Preview the 4 daily lessons to ensure you review or introduce skills that may be unfamiliar to students.

This Inventor Is All Thumbs!

Last year, ten-year-old georgia crawford set a record she became the youngest inventer [inventor] to sell a product on a network television show. After a five-minute ad about her product ran on the Shop-at-Home show sales of her product brought in $20,000 in this interview, business youth editor ivan green interviews ms. crawford (known to family and friends as Gigi) about her success in business.

MONDAY   **WEEK 29**

Error Summary	
Capitalization	10
Punctuation:	
Comma	1
Period	2
Other	1
Spelling	1

Ivan Green (IG): Ms crawford could you tell Business Youth readers about the product that you invented?

Georgia Crawford (GC): Yes mr Green but please call me Gigi. minnesota gets very cold during the winter no matter what I'd do i couldn't keep my hands warm and dry. Snow was always getting inside my gloves or mittens and I'd end up with wet freezing hands.

TUESDAY   **WEEK 29**

Error Summary	
Capitalization	5
Punctuation:	
Comma	6
Period	3
Other	2

Name _____

This Inventor Is All Thumbs!

Last year, ten-year-old georgia crawford set a record she became the youngest inventer to sell a product on a network television show. After a five-minute ad about her product ran on the Shop-at-Home show sales of her product brought in $20,000 in this interview, <u>business youth</u> editor ivan green interviews ms. crawford (known to family and friends as Gigi) about her success in business.

WATCH FOR

• titles of magazines
• titles of TV shows

MONDAY   **WEEK 29**

Ivan Green (IG): Ms crawford could you tell Business Youth readers about the product that you invented

Georgia Crawford (GC): Yes mr Green but please call me Gigi. minnesota gets very cold during the winter no matter what I'd do i couldn't keep my hands warm and dry. Snow was always getting inside my gloves or mittens and I'd end up with wet freezing hands.

WATCH FOR

■ titles of magazines
• commas

TUESDAY   **WEEK 29**

IG: So what did you do, Gigi?

GC: Well, i started pulling my long sleeves down, over my hands before I'd put on my gloves or mittens. That way, I'd have a warm layer inside my gloves to ~~seel~~ seal out the wet and cold. my mother was doing the wash one day, and she noticed that I had made a ~~whole~~ hole near the cuffs of lots of my sweaters and shirts.

Error Summary	
Capitalization	3
Punctuation:	
Apostrophe	1
Comma	2
Period	2
Other	1
Spelling	2

WEDNESDAY   **WEEK 29**

IG: Was it because of the way you were pulling on them, gigi?

GC: Yes, Mr. Green. i'd been pulling my sleeves over my hands and holding them with my thumbs. soon, I wore holes through the sleeves! That's when i realized that i needed a long-sleeved sweater or shirt, with special holes for the thumbs. Now, I sell shirts and sweaters with thumbholes. ~~their~~ They're called "Thumbkins." No more wet, cold hands!

Error Summary	
Capitalization	7
Punctuation:	
Apostrophe	1
Comma	2
Period	5
Other	1
Spelling	1

THURSDAY   **WEEK 29**

EMC 2727 • Daily Paragraph Editing, Grade 4 • ©2004 by Evan-Moor Corp.

IG: So what did you do Gigi.

GC: Well, i started pulling my long sleeves down. Over my hands before I'd put on my gloves or mittens. That way, Id have a warm layer inside my gloves to seel out the wet and cold my mother was doing the wash one day and she noticed that I had made a whole near the cuffs of lots of my sweaters and shirts.

- commas
- spelling

WEDNESDAY   **WEEK 29**

IG: Was it because of the way you were pulling on them gigi.

GC: Yes, Mr. Green i'd been pulling my sleeves over my hands and holding them with my thumbs soon, I wore holes through the sleeves! Thats when i realized that i needed a long-sleeved sweater or shirt. With special holes for the thumbs. Now, I sell shirts and sweaters with thumbholes their called "Thumbkins" No more wet cold hands!

■ commas

THURSDAY   **WEEK 29**

Preview the 4 daily lessons to ensure you review or introduce skills that may be unfamiliar to students.

Chen Wan's Vacation Diary

Monday, april 12: Spring break is going to be ~~a~~ an
exciting, different experience this year. Dads
business partner is coming to town, and he is going
to bring danny his son. They live in montana. Danny
~~have~~ has never been to california. Dad told me, Chen
Wan, I'm counting on you to show danny the city
while mr Connors and I have our business meetings"
i have been busy making plans for our days together.

Error Summary

Capitalization	7
Language Usage	2
Punctuation:	
Apostrophe	1
Comma	4
Period	3
Quotation Mark	1

MONDAY   **WEEK 30**

---

wednesday april, 14: I didnt get a chance to write
an entry yesterday, Because i was busy all day with
danny. today will be busy, ~~to~~ too. thats why Im writing
this morning before our day begins. Yesterday, we
spent most of our time in Chinatown. The ~~bildings~~ buildings
and the chinese writing everywhere ~~amaze~~ amazed danny.
He said, "Wow, I cant believe you can read these
signs, Chen Wan!"

Error Summary

Capitalization	9
Language Usage	1
Punctuation:	
Apostrophe	4
Comma	3
Period	2
Quotation Mark	1
Other	1
Spelling	2

TUESDAY   **WEEK 30**

Name _____

Chen Wan's Vacation Diary

• dialog
• commas

Monday, april 12: Spring break is going to be a exciting different experience this year. Dads business partner is coming to town and he is going to bring danny his son. They live in montana. Danny have never been to california. Dad told me, Chen Wan I'm counting on you to show danny the city while mr Connors and I have our business meetings" i have been busy making plans for our days together

MONDAY   **WEEK 30**

wednesday april, 14: I didnt get a chance to write an entry yesterday. Because i was busy all day with danny. today will be busy, to. thats why Im writing this morning before our day begins. Yesterday, we spent most of our time in Chinatown The bildings and the chinese writing everywhere amaze danny. He said, "Wow I cant believe you can read these signs Chen Wan

• apostrophes
• exclamation points

TUESDAY   **WEEK 30**

©2004 by Evan-Moor Corp. • *Daily Paragraph Editing, Grade 4* • EMC 2727   **129**

thursday April 15: Yesterday, danny and i went to Golden gate park. We had a grate (great) time at the playground, and we even rode the merry-go-round a few times. In the late afternoon, we went to see a (an) exhibit at the asian art museum, dannys favorites were the beautiful, delicate, hand-carved ivory figures. He kept saying, "Read the chinese characters, Chen Wan. it sure make (makes) me feel important to know chinese!

Error Summary

Capitalization	12
Language Usage	2
Punctuation:	
Apostrophe	1
Comma	7
Period	1
Quotation Mark	1
Other	1
Spelling	1

WEDNESDAY　　　　　　　　　　WEEK 30

Saturday, april 17: Dad and I took danny and his father to the airport this morning. Dad said he and Mr. connors were able to do everything they had hoping (hoped) to this week. At the airport, Mr. Connors said, "Chen Wan, Danny says you is (are) the best san francisco tour guide a visitor could hope to have. I think i turned red when I heard that, but i felt happy that I had helped dad. Im also happy to have a new freind (friend).

Error Summary

Capitalization	8
Language Usage	2
Punctuation:	
Apostrophe	1
Comma	3
Period	2
Quotation Mark	1
Spelling	1

THURSDAY　　　　　　　　　　WEEK 30

Name _____

thursday April 15: Yesterday, danny and i went to Golden gate park. We had a grate time at the playground and we even rode the merry-go-round a few times. In the late afternoon we went to see a exhibit at the asian art museum dannys favorites were the beautiful delicate hand-carved ivory figures. He kept saying "Read the chinese characters Chen Wan. it sure make me feel important to know chinese

• dialog
• exclamation points

WEDNESDAY   **WEEK 30**

Saturday, april 17: Dad and I took danny and his father to the airport this morning. Dad said he and Mr. connors were able to do everything they had hoping to this week. At the airport, Mr Connors said "Chen Wan Danny says you is the best san francisco tour guide a visitor could hope to have. I think i turned red when I heard that but i felt happy that I had helped dad. Im also happy to have a new freind

• dialog
• commas

THURSDAY   **WEEK 30**

Preview the 4 daily lessons to ensure you review or introduce skills that may be unfamiliar to students.

An Oregon Trail Diary

Monday, april 11 1852: after months of ~~planing~~ planning and waiting the day is almost here! the wagons are almost ~~loded~~ loaded and our journey to oregon will finally ~~began~~ begin this week. Today, I helped mother pack all the things we will need for cooking on the trail. Everything fits in a heavy sturdy ~~woodin~~ wooden box that Father built the front of the box folds down on hinges and ~~he~~ it turns into a shelf where mother can work.

Error Summary	
Capitalization	7
Language Usage	2
Punctuation:	
Comma	5
Period	2
Spelling	3

MONDAY   **WEEK 31**

---

friday April 15 1852: Amy and ~~me~~ I ~~is~~ are going to sleep in the wagon tonight we will leave before daylight. mother and father have almost ~~finnished~~ finished packing the wagon. i am going to bring this journal with me but father says I may choose only one toy to bring? It is not really difficult to ~~deside~~ decide because Amanda my rag doll is my most special toy. Grandmother made ~~him~~ her for me

Error Summary	
Capitalization	6
Language Usage	3
Punctuation:	
Comma	6
Period	3
Spelling	2

TUESDAY   **WEEK 31**

An Oregon Trail Diary

Monday, april 11 1852: after months of planing and waiting the day is almost here! the wagons are almost loded and our journey to oregon will finally began this week. Today, I helped mother pack all the things we will need. for cooking on the trail. Everything fits in a heavy sturdy woodin box that Father built the front of the box folds down on hinges and he turns into a shelf where mother can work.

- commas
- names of people

MONDAY   **WEEK 31**

friday April, 15 1852: Amy and me is going to sleep in the wagon tonight we will leave before daylight. mother and father have almost finnished packing the wagon. i am going to bring this journal with me but father says I may choose only one toy to bring? It is not really difficult to deside because Amanda my rag doll is my most special toy. Grandmother made him for me

- commas
- names of people

TUESDAY   **WEEK 31**

monday may 2 1852: We are camped on the banks of the missouri river. It is the ~~bigest~~ [biggest] river i ~~has~~ [have] ever seen! we will cross it ~~tomorow.~~ [tomorrow] First, all the wagons that arrived before us must take ~~there~~ [their] turns. I was afraid of the crossing when i first saw the river but now that Ive watched other wagons float across on the ferryboats, I think we will make it just fine. im glad that we will not cross in ~~no~~ stormy weather.

Error Summary

Capitalization	8
Language Usage	2
Punctuation:	
Apostrophe	2
Comma	4
Period	1
Spelling	3

WEDNESDAY **WEEK 31**

tuesday may 17 1852: I have not ~~groan~~ [grown] tired of looking at this prairie. no matter where I look, there are flowers blooming among the wild, waving grass. Amy and i picked a bunch for mother when ~~they~~ [we] ~~stoped~~ [stopped] for our midday meal. I will press some of the bright-yellow goldenrod here between the pages of this journal. this will save a little bit of the bright, sunny prairie along with my memories of the oregon trail.

Error Summary

Capitalization	8
Language Usage	1
Punctuation:	
Comma	5
Spelling	2

THURSDAY **WEEK 31**

monday may 2 1852: We are camped on the banks of the missouri river. It is the bigest river i has ever seen! we will cross it tomorow. First, all the wagons that arrived before us must take there turns. I was afraid of the crossing when i first saw the river but now that Ive watched other wagons float across on the ferryboats. I think we will make it just fine. im glad that we will not cross in no stormy weather

- commas
- spelling

WEDNESDAY   **WEEK 31**

tuesday may 17 1852: I have not groan tired of looking at this prairie. no matter where I look there are flowers blooming among the wild waving grass. Amy and i picked a bunch for mother when they stoped for our midday meal. I will press some of the bright-yellow goldenrod here between the pages of this journal. this will save a little bit of the bright sunny prairie along with my memories of the oregon trail.

- commas

THURSDAY   **WEEK 31**

Preview the 4 daily lessons to ensure you review or introduce skills that may be unfamiliar to students.

Why Making Maple Syrup Is Hard Work

Not so very long ago, life on earth was easy for people, sunlight warmed the land. The forests, meadows, and lakes ~~was~~ were home to countless animals. Hunters found plenty of game, and the rivers offered a bounty of fish. Berries hung ~~hevy~~ heavy on the bushes, and the cornfields grew tall. Even the trees ~~was~~ were full of sticky, sweet syrup. a broken twig provided plenty of fresh syrup right from the branch!

Error Summary	
Capitalization	3
Language Usage	2
Punctuation:	
Comma	6
Period	2
Spelling	1

MONDAY   **WEEK 32**

Nanabozho was the mighty ruler of the seasons and of nature. One day, he went for a walk to enjoy the sights, sounds, and smells of the world. when he came upon the peoples ~~vilage~~ village, though, he was surprised. There was nobody to be seen anywhere. Nanabozho found no one fishing in the stream, no hunters wandering ~~threw~~ through the woods, and nobody weeding or hoeing in the ~~cornfeild~~ cornfield. "How odd," he thought.

Error Summary	
Capitalization	1
Punctuation:	
Apostrophe	1
Comma	6
Period	1
Quotation Mark	1
Spelling	3

TUESDAY   **WEEK 32**

Name _____

Why Making Maple Syrup Is Hard Work

Not so very long ago life on earth was easy for people sunlight warmed the land. The forests meadows and lakes was home to countless animals Hunters found plenty of game and the rivers offered a bounty of fish. Berries hung hevy on the bushes and the cornfields grew tall. Even the trees was full of sticky sweet syrup. a broken twig provided plenty of fresh syrup right from the branch!

- commas

MONDAY   **WEEK 32**

Nanabozho was the mighty ruler of the seasons and of nature. One day, he went for a walk to enjoy the sights sounds and smells of the world. when he came upon the peoples vilage, though he was surprised. There was nobody to be seen anywhere Nanabozho found no one fishing in the stream no hunters wandering threw the woods and nobody weeding or hoeing in the cornfeild. "How odd he thought.

- commas
- spelling

TUESDAY   **WEEK 32**

Perhaps they are gathering berries" thought Nanabozho. As he walked toward the berry bushes however, he saw a strange sight in the maple grove He saw the people from the village but they did not see him they were lying on their backs with their mouths open. They were catching the droplets of moist sweet syrup that dripped from the trees. They did not want to get up To hunt fish or work in the fields

Error Summary

Capitalization	2
Language Usage	1
Punctuation:	
Comma	6
Period	4
Quotation Mark	1

WEDNESDAY   **WEEK 32**

Nanabozho thought to himself "This cannot be. the people will become fat and lazy. They will not want to work anymore. Soon, nanabozho had a plan he took a basket to the river. He filled the basket many times and then He emptied it over the top of a maple tree. Soon, the trees had watery flavorless sap. Since then, people must work hard To gather that thin sap and boil it down into delicious sweet syrup.

Error Summary

Capitalization	5
Language Usage	2
Punctuation:	
Comma	4
Period	2
Quotation Mark	1

THURSDAY   **WEEK 32**

Name _____

Perhaps they are gathering berries" thought Nanabozho. As he walked toward the berry bushes however, he saw a strange sight in the maple grove He saw the people from the village but they did not see him they were lying on their backs with their mouths open. They was catching the droplets of moist sweet syrup that dripped from the trees. They did not want to get up. To hunt fish or work in the fields

• commas

WEDNESDAY   **WEEK 32**

Nanabozho thought to himself "This cannot be. the people will become fat and lazy. They will not want to work anymore. Soon, nanabozho had a plan he take a basket to the river. He filled the basket many times and then He emptied her over the top of a maple tree. Soon, the trees had watery flavorless sap. Since then, people must work hard. To gather that thin sap and boil it down into delicious sweet syrup.

• commas

THURSDAY   **WEEK 32**

Preview the 4 daily lessons to ensure you review or introduce skills that may be unfamiliar to students.

"Hot Sauce" Is Sizzling!

Error Summary

Capitalization	4
Language Usage	1
Punctuation:	
Apostrophe	1
Comma	4
Period	3
Other	1

Miami florida   july 19 2004

Have you heard? Some fresh new voices are making lots of noise these days in the world of music the teenage brother and sister calls [call] themselves Hot Sauce and everyone says their music is sizzling? Its no surprise that twins Eva and Alex Cruz feel at home onstage? And in the recording studio. Both of their parents are performers.

MONDAY   **WEEK 33**

The new hit by hot sauce is a lively song called "Nice and Spicy." The tune shows off the musical talents of the duo according to the twins they have spent many tedious hard hours over the past year on lessons practice and rehearsals. The hard work seems to have payed [paid] off. alex sounds great on the guitar and eva does some fine work on the keyboard This duo has a long career ahead of them?!

Error Summary

Capitalization	5
Punctuation:	
Comma	5
Period	2
Other	1
Spelling	1

TUESDAY   **WEEK 33**

Name _____

"Hot Sauce" Is Sizzling!

Miami florida   july 19 2004

     Have you heard. Some fresh new voices are making lots of noise these days in the world of music the teenage brother and sister calls themselves Hot Sauce and everyone says their music is sizzling? Its no surprise that twins Eva and Alex Cruz feel at home onstage. And in the recording studio. Both of their parents are performers.

• commas

MONDAY   **WEEK 33**

     The new hit by hot sauce is a lively song called "Nice and Spicy." The tune shows off the musical talents of the duo according to the twins they have spent many tedious hard hours over the past year on lessons practice and rehearsals. The hard work seems to have payed off. alex sounds great on the guitar and eva does some fine work on the keyboard This duo has a long career ahead of them?

• commas

TUESDAY   **WEEK 33**

According to the cruz family the hard work doesn't end once a recording becomes a hit. In fact, that's when a totally ~~diferent~~ different kind of work ~~begin~~ begins Eva Alex and their parents will now spend several busy action-packed weeks touring big ~~citys~~ cities across the united states. There will be interviews concerts, talk shows and fans everywhere Hot sauce will sing Nice and Spicy on the television show Young Talent.

Error Summary

Capitalization	4
Language Usage	1
Punctuation:	
Apostrophe	1
Comma	6
Period	2
Quotation Mark	2
Other	1
Spelling	2

WEDNESDAY   **WEEK 33**

If hot sauce continues to have big hits like Nice And Spicy we may be seeing them on TV again later this year. Sources in the music world ~~says~~ say that hot sauce may win a music award for Nice and spicy. If so, count on seeing Eva and Alex Cruz on TV in the Young Music Awards program next season. In the meantime, ~~keap~~ keep an eye on this hot duo because they show no signs of cooling off any time soon!

Error Summary

Capitalization	6
Language Usage	1
Punctuation:	
Comma	1
Quotation Mark	4
Other	1
Spelling	2

THURSDAY   **WEEK 33**

EMC 2727 • Daily Paragraph Editing, Grade 4 • ©2004 by Evan-Moor Corp.

Name _____

According to the cruz family the hard work doesn't end once a recording becomes a hit. In fact, thats when a totally diferent kind of work begin Eva Alex and their parents will now spend several busy action-packed weeks touring big citys across the united states. There will be interviews concerts, talk shows and fans everywhere Hot sauce will sing Nice and Spicy on the television show Young Talent.

- titles of songs
- titles of TV shows

WEDNESDAY   **WEEK 33**

If hot sauce continues to have big hits like Nice And Spicy we may be seeing them on TV again later this year. Sources in the music world says that hot sauce may win a music award for Nice and spicy. If so, count on seeing Eva and Alex Cruz on TV in the Young Music Awards program next season. In the meantime, keap an eye on this hot duo because they show no signs of cooling off any time soon!

- titles of songs
- titles of TV shows

THURSDAY   **WEEK 33**

Preview the 4 daily lessons to ensure you review or introduce skills that may be unfamiliar to students.

A Weather Journal

november 5 2004   1:30 pm.

    Yesterday, ms chan handed out weather journals to each science team. we will be ~~studyng~~ studying the weather for a couple of weeks each team got special tools for checking the weather. ms chan gave us ~~an~~ a thermometer a rain gauge and a windsock we will measure how hot or cold the air is with the thermometer check the rainfall with the gauge and find out the direction of the wind with the windsock

Error Summary	
Capitalization	8
Language Usage	1
Punctuation:	
Comma	5
Period	6
Spelling	1

MONDAY   **WEEK 34**

november 6 2004   ~~14:5~~ 1:45 pm

    Our ~~sience~~ science team is made up of nelson pat paula and me. yesterday, we set up our weather tools The thermometer is tacked to the back wall of the cafeteria and the rain gauge is in the ground at the edge of the field It ~~look~~ looks like a tall cup attached to ~~an~~ a stick. Our windsock is on a pole and it's in the ground, ~~to.~~ too Our thermometer says 61°F there isnt any rain falling and the wind is blowing from the north

Error Summary	
Capitalization	6
Language Usage	2
Punctuation:	
Apostrophe	2
Comma	8
Period	6
Other	1
Spelling	2

TUESDAY   **WEEK 34**

Name _____

A Weather Journal

november 5 2004   1:30 pm.

    Yesterday, ms chan handed out weather journals to each science team. we will be studyng the weather for a couple of weeks each team got special tools for checking the weather. ms chan gave us an thermometer a rain gauge and a windsock we will measure how hot or cold the air is with the thermometer check the rainfall with the gauge and find out the direction of the wind with the windsock

- abbreviations

MONDAY   **WEEK 34**

november, 6 2004   14:5 pm

    Our sience team is made up of nelson pat paula and me. yesterday, we set up our weather tools The thermometer is tacked to the back wall of the cafeteria and the rain gauge is in the ground at the edge of the field It look like a tall cup attached to an stick. Our windsock is on a pole and its in the ground, to. Our thermometer says 61°F there isnt any rain falling and the wind is blowing from the north

- colons in time
- commas

TUESDAY   **WEEK 34**

Nov. 7, 2004   10:15 a.m.

    Dark patches began to cover the sky at dusk last night then it started to rain and continued all night. This morning, Ms. chan sent us out to check our weather station our rain gauge had 0.75 in. of water in it! Juan's group only had 0.25 in. of rain in their gauge but they put it under an awning. Our gauge was completely uncovered the air is now 59°F. and the windsock is blowing in a northerly direction.

Error Summary

Capitalization	4
Language Usage	1
Punctuation:	
Apostrophe	1
Comma	3
Period	6
Other	1

WEDNESDAY   **WEEK 34**

Nov. 8, 2004   2:30 pm.

    It has been windy today but it hasn't been raining our windsock is flying straight out. We're not sure if the wind is coming from the north. Or the northeast. We are sure about how much rain is in our rain gauge we had 1.25 in. this afternoon. Susans group had 1 in. at 10:15 a.m. Juan's group only had 0.75 in. at 1:30 pm. Ms. chan wants us to figure out why we all got different amounts. I have some ideas.

Error Summary

Capitalization	5
Punctuation:	
Apostrophe	3
Comma	1
Period	11
Other	1
Spelling	1

THURSDAY   **WEEK 34**

Name _____

Nov. 7 2004   10.15 a.m

     Dark patches began to cover the sky at dusk last night then it started to rain and continued all night. This morning, Ms chan sent us out to check our weather station our rain gauge had 0.75 in. of water in it! Juans group only had 0.25 in of rain in their gauge but they put it under a awning. Our gauge was completely uncovered the air is now 59°F and the windsock is blowing in a northerly direction.

• abbreviations
• colons in time

WEDNESDAY   **WEEK 34**

Nov 8, 2004   2'30 pm

     It has been windy today but it hasn't been raining our windsock is flying strait out. Were not sure if the wind is coming from the north. Or the northeast. We are sure about how much rain is in our rain gauge we had 1.25 in this afternoon. susans group had 1 in at 10:15 a.m. Juans group only had 0.75 in at 1:30 pm. Ms. chan wants us to figure out why we all got different amounts I have some ideas.

• abbreviations
• colons in time

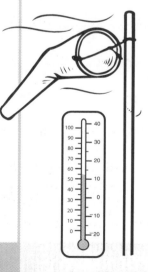

THURSDAY   **WEEK 34**

Preview the 4 daily lessons to ensure you review or introduce skills that may be unfamiliar to students.

How to Make Napkin Rings

Nothing makes ~~an~~ a holiday table more festive ~~then~~ than special napkin rings? they are simple to make, and they add so much to a holiday meal you will need to have cardboard tubes from paper towels, paper (wrapping paper, self-stick paper, or paper you have decorated), glue, scissors, a pen or pencil, a ruler, and any extra decorations you want to include. ~~Stikkers~~ Stickers are great for this project.

Error Summary	
Capitalization	2
Language Usage	1
Punctuation:	
Comma	8
Period	3
Spelling	2

MONDAY   **WEEK 35**

First, use the ruler to make a mark at every inch on the paper towel tube. second, cut along each ~~eatch~~ mark to create cardboard rings. if you dont have a ring for each of your guests, ~~repete~~ repeat these steps with another tube. Next, cut strips of paper that measure two ~~to~~ and one-half inches wide and five and one-half inches long. Youll need one of these strips, for each of the rings you ~~plans~~ plan to make.

Error Summary	
Capitalization	2
Language Usage	1
Punctuation:	
Apostrophe	2
Comma	1
Period	1
Other	1
Spelling	3

TUESDAY   **WEEK 35**

Name _____

How to Make Napkin Rings

Nothing makes an holiday table more festive then special napkin rings? they are simple to make and they add so much to a holiday meal you will need to have cardboard tubes from paper towels paper (wrapping paper self-stick paper or paper you have decorated), glue scissors a pen or pencil a ruler and any extra decorations you want to include. Stikkers are great for this project

- commas

MONDAY   **WEEK 35**

First, use the ruler to make a mark at every inch on the paper towel tube. second, cut along eatch mark to create cardboard rings. if you dont have a ring for each of your guests repete these steps with another tube. Next, cut strips of paper that measure to and one-half inches wide and five and one half inches long. Youll need one of these strips. for each of the rings you plans to make.

- hyphens in fractions
- spelling

TUESDAY   **WEEK 35**

Spread
~~spred~~ glue on the outside of a cardboard ring.
center the ring on one end of a strip of paper
and ~~role~~ roll the paper around it? There should be
three-quarters of an inch of paper left over. On
each side of the ring. Make cuts in the paper on
each side of the tube, about one-half inch apart. Rub
glue
~~glew~~ inside the ring then fold the strips of paper
toward the inside of the ring.

Error Summary

Capitalization	4
Punctuation:	
Period	4
Other	2
Spelling	3

WEDNESDAY   **WEEK 35**

Now that your ring is covered with paper, you
may add ribbon, glitter, self-hardening clay, or any
other decoration you wish. When the set of napkin
finished
rings is ~~finish~~, use them for a special meal. just roll
a paper or cloth napkin, tuck it through a ring, and
set
then ~~sit~~ it. On the table alongside the plate. Keep the
Rings in a box or bag so you can use them again for
other special occasions.

Error Summary

Capitalization	3
Language Usage	1
Punctuation:	
Comma	6
Period	3
Spelling	1

THURSDAY   **WEEK 35**

spred glue on the outside of a cardboard ring. center the ring on one end of a strip of paper and role the paper around it? There should be three quarters of an inch of paper left over. On each side of the ring. Make cuts in the paper on each side of the tube, about one half inch apart Rub glew inside the ring then fold the strips of paper toward the inside of the ring.

- hyphens in fractions
- spelling

WEDNESDAY   **WEEK 35**

Now that your ring is covered with paper you may add ribbon glitter self-hardening clay or any other decoration you wish. When the set of napkin rings is finish use them for a special meal just roll a paper or cloth napkin tuck it through a ring, and then sit it. On the table alongside the plate. Keep the Rings in a box or bag so you can use them again for other special occasions

- commas

THURSDAY   **WEEK 35**

Preview the 4 daily lessons to ensure you review or introduce skills that may be unfamiliar to students.

How to Make Stilts

Have you ever tried to walk on stilts? Its harder than it looks, but its lots of fun. walking on stilts can improve your balance its also a great way to be head and shoulders above the ~~croud~~ crowd in a parade! In fact, in the early 1700s, french shepherds used stilts to keep an eye on their flocks. Stilts are easy to make? Ask a adult to help you find the materials listed below, then follow the directions.

an

Error Summary	
Capitalization	4
Language Usage	1
Punctuation:	
Apostrophe	3
Comma	2
Period	4
Other	1
Spelling	1

MONDAY   **WEEK 36**

You will need wood, a tape measure, a hammer, a saw, wood glue, and ~~nailes~~ nails. To make the handles for your stilts, you will need two 6-foot lengths of lumber (1 in. thick by 2 in. wide). for your stilt's steps, you will need two 10-inch lengths of lumber (2 in. thick by 4 in. wide). Finally, you will need sandpaper to smooth the handles? you may wish to ~~paynte~~ paint your stilts when they are finished.

Error Summary	
Capitalization	2
Punctuation:	
Comma	5
Period	5
Spelling	2

TUESDAY   **WEEK 36**

Name _____

How to Make Stilts

Have you ever tried to walk on stilts. Its harder than it looks but its lots of fun. walking on stilts can improve your balance its also a great way to be head and shoulders above the croud in a parade! In fact, in the early 1700s french shepherds used stilts to keep an eye on their flocks. Stilts are easy to make? Ask a adult to help you find the materials listed below then follow the directions

WATCH FOR

- run-on sentences
- apostrophes

You will need wood, a tape measure a hammer a saw wood glue, and nailes. To make the handles for your stilts you will need two 6-foot lengths of lumber (1 in. thick by 2 in wide). for your stilt's steps you will need two 10-inch lengths of lumber (2 in thick by 4 in wide). Finally, you will need sandpaper to smooth the handles? you may wish to paynte your stilts. when they are finished.

WATCH FOR

- abbreviations
- commas

To make the handles, first ask your helper to measure the distance, From the ~~grownd~~ (ground) to the top of your shoulders. Second, add 1 foot, to this measurement. Next, cut the two 6-foot lengths of lumber to this measurement. ~~Finaly,~~ (Finally,) sand them carefully with the sandpaper, you want to make sure there are ~~know~~ (no) splinters. It's hard enough to balance on stilts without having to ~~worried~~ (worry) about slivers!

Error Summary

Capitalization	2
Language Usage	1
Punctuation:	
Apostrophe	1
Comma	1
Period	3
Spelling	3

WEDNESDAY   **WEEK 36**

To make the steps, first ~~spred~~ (spread) wood glue on one long side of each of the 10-inch lengths of lumber. Second, attach the steps to the bottom of the handles. Next, use the hammer to drive ~~for~~ (four) nails, Through each handle and into the step. If you want to make your stilts more ~~colorfull,~~ (colorful,) wait until the glue is completely dry and then paint them. Let the paint dry now. ~~your~~ (you're) ready to practice walking on your stilts!

Error Summary

Capitalization	2
Punctuation:	
Comma	2
Period	3
Spelling	4

THURSDAY   **WEEK 36**

Name _____

To make the handles first ask your helper to measure the distance. From the grownd to the top of your shoulders. Second, add 1 foot. to this measurement. Next, cut the two 6-foot lengths of lumber to this measurement. Finaly, sand them carefully with the sandpaper you want to make sure there are know splinters. Its hard enough to balance on stilts without having to worried about slivers!

WATCH FOR

• spelling

WEDNESDAY   **WEEK 36**

To make the steps first spred wood glue on one long side of each of the 10-inch lengths of lumber. Second, attach the steps to the bottom of the handles Next, use the hammer to drive for nails. Through each handle and into the step. If you want to make your stilts more colorfull wait until the glue is completely dry and then paint them. Let the paint dry now your ready to practice walking on your stilts!

WATCH FOR

• spelling

THURSDAY   **WEEK 36**

Write a paragraph that gives information about kites. Write your own topic sentence, or choose one provided below. Don't forget to add examples or details about the topic.

- Did you know that kites have been used to do important jobs as well as for having fun?

- People have been making and using kites for over two thousand years.

- All over the world, people make and fly kites.

Write a paragraph that describes the work that was done by Gregor Mendel. Tell about at least one important thing that was learned from his work. Begin with one of these topic sentences, or write your own:

- Gregor Mendel's work has helped scientists understand how traits are passed from parents to children.

- Gregor Mendel's work with plants has also helped scientists understand humans better.

- Does it seem possible that studying plants could help us learn about people?

Do you think school uniforms are a good idea? Write a persuasive paragraph about this issue. Be sure to clearly state whether you support this idea. Give at least three reasons to support your position. End with a strong closing sentence.

Write a short letter to a real or imaginary friend. Describe what you are doing in school these days, or tell about something that is going on in your life.

Letters: Pen Pals

Imagine you are having a birthday party. Write an invitation to a friend. Be sure to tell the date, time, and place of your party. Add any other details that you want to include.

Letters: Birthday Mail

Write the last paragraph of this story, telling what the letter says and how the writer feels about the news. Use the same voice as the narrator of the first four paragraphs.

Realistic Fiction: The Letter

Write another paragraph about life in Salinas, Alta California. Describe some of the children's other chores, like working in the garden, carding wool, herding sheep, gathering eggs, or other tasks. Continue writing in the same voice as the author of the other four paragraphs.

Write a paragraph that summarizes important information about Lewis and Clark's exploration of the Louisiana Territory. Be sure to include information about when the group made the trip, the reasons for the trip, who took part in the trip, and the outcome of the journey.

Write one or two paragraphs about the Everglades. Explain what makes this place special. Describe the problems facing the Everglades today. Close with a strong concluding statement. Begin with one of these topic sentences, or write your own:

- A special ecosystem like the Everglades deserves to be protected.

- People's actions can upset the delicate balance of a habitat.

- One of America's most unusual areas is the Everglades in Florida.

Write a paragraph to summarize the information about Herrington and his November 2002 mission to the International Space Station. Begin with one of these topic sentences, or write your own:

- Astronaut John Herrington took more than scientific equipment with him on his trip to outer space.

- Astronaut John Herrington is the first Native American to go into space.

- The Chickasaw Nation gave a proud send-off to Native American astronaut John Herrington.

FRIDAY – WEEK 10   **Science Article: Arrowheads in Space**

Describe the two huge memorials in South Dakota. Be sure to tell who designed them, what they represent, and when they were made. Begin with one of these topic sentences, or write your own:

- South Dakota is home to two of the largest memorials in the world.

- South Dakota's granite cliffs are perfect for carving monuments.

- Sometimes, big ideas can become big projects.

FRIDAY – WEEK 11   **Social Studies Article: A Monumental Tribute**

Write one or two paragraphs that describe a place that is special to you. What does it look like and sound like there? How do you feel when you are there? What makes it such a special place?

FRIDAY – WEEK 12   **Personal Narrative: My Tree House**

The Gold Rush was an important time in California's history. In one or two paragraphs, write a summary that describes events related to the Gold Rush. Remember to include details about the way miners panned for gold and claimed land. Begin with one of the following topic sentences, or write one of your own:

- The Gold Rush began in 1848 when a man named James Marshall found a gold nugget.

- Many forty-niners looked for their fortune in the American River.

- In 1848, many people began their journey to California with dreams of striking it rich.

FRIDAY – WEEK 13   **Social Studies Article: Gold!**

Write a paragraph that tells about where electrical energy comes from and how it is used. Begin with one of these topic sentences, or write your own:

- Most people are used to having electrical power available at the flip of a switch.

- Have you ever wondered where the electrical energy in your home comes from?

- Electrical energy can be made in different ways.

FRIDAY – WEEK 14   **Science Article: Electric Energy**

Write one or two paragraphs about the life and work of Marie Curie. Be sure to include where and when she was born, and to describe some of the things that made her an extraordinary person. Use one of these topic sentences to begin, or write your own:

- Marie Curie was an inspiring woman and scientist.

- Marie Curie helped make some important discoveries in the world of science.

- Marie Curie spent her life studying, learning, and discovering.

FRIDAY – WEEK 15   **Biography: A Woman of Science**

Write a paragraph that *gives information about teeth and the work they do.* Begin with one of these topic sentences, or write your own:

- Teeth have different shapes because they do different jobs.

- It's important to take care of your teeth so they can do their job.

- What is a tool that can cut, grind, and tear?

Write a paragraph describing how new technology has changed the way people find information. Be sure to give some examples. Begin with one of these topic sentences, or write your own:

- The Internet has become a one-stop source of information for many people.

- Do you know one place where you can find a weather report, buy tickets to a ballgame, or research a topic for school?

- Computers have changed a lot in recent decades.

Write a paragraph describing a day spent with your family, or tell about how you spend a day on the weekend. Use your words to help paint a vivid picture for your readers.

Write one or two paragraphs that tell about something that you did or that happened to you. You can tell about something that happened recently, or when you were small. Help the reader understand what happened and how you felt about it.

Use the information in the book review to write a summary of <u>Little House on the Prairie</u>. Be sure to tell what type of book this is, where and when the story takes place, and who wrote it. Include some information on what the book is about. You might also give a recommendation.

Write one or two paragraphs to continue this story. Tell what happens after Robin starts working on Grow-Bot, the robotic tutor. Is the project a success? Is it a new, interesting form of entertainment? Or do things get out of control and create a disaster? What might happen? Include some dialog between speakers in the story. Be sure to use capital letters, quotation marks, and punctuation correctly when you write dialog.

Suggest other activities that schools could plan for the rest of an environmental awareness week. Present convincing arguments for the activities you propose for Wednesday, Thursday, and Friday. Give examples of environmental problems, and explain how the ideas you suggest would contribute to solving them. Be sure to end with a strong concluding statement.

Write a paragraph that describes the pirate Blackbeard. Be sure to tell about the way he looked and acted. Share some other interesting information about the pirate and his life. Start with one of the following topic sentences, or write your own:

- Blackbeard the Pirate knew just how to make himself look fearsome.

- In the early 1700s, the sailor Edward Teach transformed himself into Blackbeard the Pirate.

Write one or two paragraphs about the life of Maria Tallchief. Explain what made her special. Give details and use examples to create a picture of this gifted ballerina. Begin with one of these topic sentences, or write your own:

- Maria Tallchief had a rich cultural heritage that made her unique.

- Maria Tallchief was gifted in music and dance from an early age.

- America's first world-class ballerina was born on an Indian reservation in Oklahoma in 1925.

Based on the information in the book review, describe <u>Sarah Roth and the Wisdom Crystal</u>. Be sure to tell what type of book this is, who the main characters are, what the setting is, and something about the plot. Also give some information on the author. Finally, based on what you read in the book review, give your opinion about whether you think this would be an interesting book to read.

Write a one-paragraph version of the news story about the <u>Prestige</u> oil spill. Be sure to tell what happened, and when and where the events occurred. Choose one of these headlines, or write your own:

- Spanish Fishing Waters at Risk

- Threat of World's Worst Oil Spill

- Experts Seek Solution to Spill

Write a paragraph that explains how people's ideas about Earth have changed over time. Be sure to give some examples. Begin with one of these topic sentences, or write your own:

- People's ideas about Earth have changed very slowly.

- Scientists now know much more about Earth than in the past.

- Is it hard to believe that some of Earth's continents used to be joined together?

Write another paragraph for Bridget's story. Tell about what happens when the ship finally arrives in Boston after six weeks at sea. Include some words spoken by Bridget, Paul, Mary, or Uncle James. Be sure to use capital letters, quotation marks, and punctuation correctly when you write dialog.

FRIDAY – WEEK 28   **Historical Fiction: A Journey Begins**

Write one or two more questions and answers for this interview. Ivan Green might ask *Gigi* to describe how she felt after selling $20,000 worth of "Thumbkins" after her ad ran on the <u>Shop-at-Home</u> show. He might ask her if she has had ideas for other inventions, or about how she will use the money she earns. Or, make up a question of your own to ask and answer.

FRIDAY – WEEK 29   **Interview: This Inventor Is All Thumbs!**

Write a journal entry for Friday, April 16. Write as if you are Chen Wan, and describe your activities with Danny. You could describe your outing to the movies on Thursday, or tell about something you did earlier in the day on Friday.

FRIDAY – WEEK 30   **Journal Entries: Chen Wan's Vacation Diary**

Write another journal entry about experiences on the Oregon Trail. You might want to imagine the day the family saw Chimney Rock (a 325-foot-tall rock formation in Nebraska) or crossed the Snake River in Idaho by ferry. Tell about sights and sounds that the writer might have seen, such as wild animals, plants, or people.

FRIDAY – WEEK 31   **Journal Entries: An Oregon Trail Diary**

This story was written to teach an important lesson. What do you think that lesson is? Write a paragraph or two to explain your ideas. Be sure to support your ideas with logic or examples.

FRIDAY – WEEK 32   **Fable: Why Making Maple Syrup Is Hard Work**

Write a news story describing one of the concerts given by Hot Sauce during their U.S. tour. Be sure to mention when and where the concert took place, as well as some of the highlights of the show. You might want to give some information about the performers, or comment on the weak points of the show.

FRIDAY – WEEK 33   **News Article: "Hot Sauce" Is Sizzling!**

Write another entry for the group's science journal for November 9th. It will be an answer to Ms. Chan's question to the class. Present an idea about why three different science teams got three different measurements when they checked their rain gauges. Use the same writing voice as the writer of the journal entries for Nov. 5 through 8.

Write step-by-step directions for using napkin rings. Be sure to explain how to arrange the napkin in the ring and exactly where to place it on the table. Use words to help signal the order of each step, such as *first*, *next*, and *finally*.

Write directions that tell how to make a pair of stilts. You may use numerals to list the steps in order or use words like *first*, *second*, *next*, and *finally* to order your directions.

Language Handbook

Basic Rules for Writing and Editing

=== Contents ===

EMC 2727 • Daily Paragraph Editing • ©2004 by Evan-Moor Corp.

Capital Letters

A word that starts with a **capital letter** is special in some way.

Always use a **capital letter** to begin:

the first word of a sentence:	Today is the first day of school.
the first word of a quotation:	She said, "Today is the first day of school."
the salutation (greeting) and closing in a letter:	Dear Grandma, Thanks so much for the birthday gift! Love, Sherry
the names of days, months, and holidays:	The fourth Thursday in November is Thanksgiving.
people's first and last names, their initials, and their titles:	Mrs. Cruz and her son Felix were both seen by Dr. S. C. Lee. **Note:** Many titles can be abbreviated. Use these abbreviations only when you also use the person's name: **Mr.** a man **Capt.** a captain **Mrs.** a married woman **Lt.** a lieutenant **Ms.** a woman **Pres.** the president of a country **Dr.** a doctor or an organization
a word that is used as a name:	I went with Dad and Aunt Terry to visit Grandma. **Be Careful!** Do not use a capital letter at the beginning of a word when it is not used as someone's name: I went with my dad and my aunt to visit my grandma. **Hint:** If you can replace the word with a name, it needs a capital letter: I went with <u>Dad</u>. ⟶ I went with <u>Joe</u>.
the word that names yourself - **I**:	My family and I enjoy camping together.

the names of nationalities and languages:	**M**exican, **C**uban, and **N**icaraguan people all speak **S**panish.
the names of racial, ethnic, or cultural groups:	There were **A**sian, **N**ative **A**merican, and **A**frican dancers at the festival.
the names of ships, planes, and space vehicles:	The president flew on **Air Force One** to see the **USS Abraham Lincoln**, a U.S. Navy aircraft carrier. **Note:** You must also underline the name of a ship, plane, or space vehicle: **the space shuttle Columbia**

to begin the names of these special places and things:	
• street names:	**P**alm **A**venue, **C**ypress **S**treet, **P**ine **B**oulevard
• cities, states, and countries:	**L**os Angeles, **C**alifornia, **U**nited **S**tates of **A**merica, **P**aris, **F**rance
• continents:	**A**sia, **E**urope, **S**outh **A**merica
• landforms and bodies of water:	**G**reat **P**lains, **S**an **F**rancisco **B**ay, **G**reat **S**alt **L**ake
• buildings, monuments, and public places:	the **W**hite **H**ouse, the **S**tatue of **L**iberty, **Y**ellowstone **N**ational **P**ark
• historic events:	The **G**old **R**ush began in 1849. The **C**ivil **W**ar ended in 1865.

Capital Letters (continued)

| titles of books, stories, poems, and magazines: | The story "The Friendly Fruit Bat" appeared in <u>Ranger Rick</u> magazine and in a science book called <u>Flying Mammals</u>.

Be Careful! Do not use a capital letter at the beginning of a small word in a title, such as **a**, **an**, **at**, **for**, **in**, and **the**, unless it is the first word in the title.

Note: When you write a title, remember . . .

Some titles are underlined:
    Book Titles: <u>Frog and Toad</u>
    Magazine Titles: <u>Ranger Rick</u>
    Movie Titles: <u>Bambi</u>
    TV Shows: <u>Sesame Street</u>
    Newspapers: <u>The Daily News</u>

Some titles go inside quotation marks:
    Story Titles: "The Fox and the Crow"
    Chapter Titles: "In Which Piglet Meets a Heffalump"
    Poem Titles: "My Shadow"
    Song Titles: "Twinkle, Twinkle, Little Star"
    Titles of Articles: "Ship Sinks in Bay" |

Punctuation Marks

Punctuation gives information that helps you understand a sentence.

End Punctuation
Every sentence must end with one of these three punctuation marks: **. ! ?**

A **period** (**.**) shows that a sentence is:

giving information:	I love to read short stories.

giving a mild command:	Choose a short story to read aloud.
	
	Note: A period is also used in:
	• abbreviations of months and days:
	   Jan. (January), Feb. (February), Mon. (Monday), etc.
	• abbreviations of measurements:
	   ft. (foot/feet), in. (inch/inches),
	   lb./lbs. (pound/pounds), oz. (ounce/ounces)
	• time:
	   8:00 a.m., 4:30 p.m., etc.

A **question mark** (**?**) shows that a sentence is:

asking a question:	Did you choose a story to read**?**

An **exclamation point** (**!**) shows that a sentence is:

expressing strong feelings:	Wow**!** That story is really long**!**

Comma

A **comma** (**,**) can help you know how to read things. Commas are often used in sentences. Sometimes commas are used with words or phrases.

Some commas are used to keep things separate. Use a **comma** to separate:

the name of a city from the name of a state:	El Paso**,** Texas
the name of a city from the name of a country:	London**,** England
the date from the year:	October 12**,** 2004
the salutation (greeting) from the body of a letter:	Dear Ms. Silver**,**
the closing in a letter from the signature:	Yours truly**,**

two adjectives that tell about the same noun:	Nico is a witty**,** smart boy.
	
	Hint: To see if you need a comma between two adjectives, use these two "tests":
	
	1 Switch the order of the adjectives. If the sentence still makes sense, you must use a comma:
	
	    YES: Nico is a witty, smart boy. ⟶ Nico is a smart, witty boy.
	
	    NO: Nico has dark brown hair. ⟶ Nico has brown dark hair.
	
	2 Put the word "and" between the two adjectives. If the sentence still makes sense, you must use a comma:
	
	    YES: Nico is a witty, smart boy. ⟶ Nico is a witty and smart boy.
	
	    NO: Nico has dark brown hair. ⟶ Nico has dark and brown hair.

Some commas help you know where to pause when you read a sentence. Use a **comma** to show a pause:

between three or more items in a list or series:	Nico won't eat beets, spinach, or shrimp.
after or before the name of a person that someone is talking to in a sentence:	**After:** Nico, I think that you need to eat more. **Before:** I think that you need to eat more, Nico. **Both:** I think, Nico, that you need to eat more.
between the words spoken by someone and the rest of the sentence:	Mrs. Flores said, "It's time to break the piñata now!" "I know," answered Maya.
after an exclamation at the beginning of a sentence:	Boy, that's a lot of candy!
after a short introductory phrase or clause that comes before the main idea:	After all that candy, nobody was hungry for cake.
before and after a word or words that interrupt the main idea of a sentence:	The cake, however, was already out on the picnic table.
before and after a word or phrase that renames or gives more information about the noun before it:	The cake, which had thick chocolate frosting, melted in the hot sun. Mrs. Lutz, our neighbor, gave Mom the recipe.
before the connecting word in a compound sentence:	The frosting was melted, but the cake was great. **Note:** A simple sentence always includes a <u>subject</u> and a <u>verb</u>, and it expresses a complete thought. A compound sentence joins two simple sentences together, so each of the two parts of a compound sentence has its own <u>subject</u> and <u>verb</u>. The two parts of a compound sentence are joined by a comma and a conjunction. The conjunctions **and**, **but**, **for**, **nor**, **or**, **so**, and **yet** are all used to join two simple sentences into one compound sentence. In a compound sentence, always place the comma before the connecting conjunction: <u>Maya</u> <u>ate</u> candy, **but** <u>she</u> <u>was</u> too full to eat cake. <u>Nico</u> <u>ate</u> candy, **and** <u>he</u> also <u>ate</u> a piece of cake. <u>Nico</u> <u>is</u> thin, **yet** <u>he</u> <u>eats</u> lots of sweets. <u>Maya</u> <u>is</u> chubby, **so** <u>she</u> <u>watches</u> what she eats.

Quotation Marks

Use **quotation marks** (" "):

before and after words that are spoken by someone:	"This was the best birthday party ever!" Maya said. **Note:** Punctuation that follows the speaker's words goes inside the quotation marks: "May I have a piñata at my birthday party?" Martin asked. Mr. Flores replied, "You bet!" **Be Careful!** When the words that tell who is speaking come before the quotation, put the comma outside the quotation marks. When the words that tell who is speaking come after the quotation, put the comma inside the quotation marks: **Before:** Mrs. Flores asked, "Do you want a chocolate cake, too?" **After:** "I sure do," said Martin.
around words that are being discussed:	The word "piñata" is written with a special letter.
around slang or words used in an unusual way:	We all had to "chill out" after the party.

Hyphen

Use a **hyphen** (–):

between numbers in a fraction:	One-half of the candies had walnuts, and one-quarter had almonds.
to join two words that work together to make an adjective before a noun:	It's not easy to find low-fat candy and sugar-free soda.

 EMC 2727 • Daily Paragraph Editing • ©2004 by Evan-Moor Corp.